Unsolved Disappearances in the Great Smoky Mountains

Juanitta Baldwin
and
Ester Grubb

D0888236

Unsolved Disappearances in the Great Smoky Mountains

Juanitta Baldwin
and
Ester Grubb

Suntop Press
Division of Suntop, Inc.
Kodak, Tennessee
Virginia Beach, Virginia

Printed and bound in the United States of America
First printing 1998 - Updated 2009 - Nineteenth Printing

Library of Congress Cataloging-in-Publication Data

Baldwin, Juanitta
        Unsolved disappearances in the Great Smoky Mountains /
Juanitta Baldwin and Ester Grubb
                p.   cm.
    ISBN 1-880309-13-4
    1. Great Smoky Mountains Region (N.C. and Tenn.) -- History
Anecdotes. 2. Great Smoky Mountains Region (N.C. and Tenn.)
Biography--Anecdotes. 3. Missing persons--Great Smoky
Mountains Region (N.C. and Tenn.) Anecdotes. 1. Grubb, Ester
II. Title
   F443.G7B35 1998
   976.8'89--dc21   98-26168

                                                CIP

TABLE OF CONTENTS

About this Book

This book began with a list of over one hundred names of persons who had met with some type of misfortune in the Great Smoky Mountains. The stories of seven of these persons are in this book.

We searched for surviving family members of each person we were writing about except William Bradford Bishop, Jr., and Eric Robert Rudolph. Our purpose was to let them know about this book so it would not be a surprise should they see it, and to give them an opportunity to tell us anything they wanted us to know. It took over two years, but we located at least one family member of each person.

We thank each person who has contacted us with information and comments since the initial publication of this book. Several persons shared information, but did not want to be identified by name. Their reasons ranged from a desire for privacy to caution about offending someone. All such requests have been circumspectly honored.

As we worked on this book, each name became a real person. We completed it with a keen hope that the unsolved disappearances will be solved during our lifetimes. It would be a joy to write the endings to these fascinating stories.

We do not consider this an irrational hope because a mystery is only a mystery to those who do not know what happened. Probabilities are high that there are people who know what happened to each person. One day one or more of them may break their silence.

About the Authors

Juanitta Baldwin is a psychologist and writer. Among her current works are *Smoky Mountain Mysteries, Smoky Mountain Ghostlore, and Smoky Mountain Tales, Volumes I and II.*

All her books are sold at http://www.amazon.com

* * * * *

Ester Grubb is a professional photographer, and certified physical education teacher.

* * * * *

This book is sold in all the Visitor Centers in the Great Smoky Mountains National Park, and online at:

http://www.smokiesstore.org

Proceeds go to the preservation of the Park.

Prologue

The Great Smoky Mountains National Park is the most visited national park in the United States.

The number of persons who meet with any type of misfortune in the Great Smoky Mountains is a finite fraction of the total number of persons there at any hour of the day or night, in any season. We hope no one will shy away from the grandeur and beauty of the Smokies because of apprehension about safety.

The Great Smoky Mountains National Park offers free information on how to visit the mountains safely.

The mailing address is 1420 Little River Road, Gatlinburg, Tennessee 37738.

There is also an abundance of reliable, current information on the Internet, and from travel agents.

* * * * *

The places where the events in this book occurred are real. You can visit them. We have included information about the specific sites, some more detailed than others.

There is a map of the Great Smoky Mountains National Park on the last page of this book. We have marked the unsolved disappearance sites on it.

If you visit any of these sites, you will leave more amazed and mystified that the event occurred than mere words can ever convey.

Part I
Vanished Without a Trace

* * * * *

Thelma Pauline (Polly) Melton

Trenny Lynn Gibson

Dennis Lloyd Martin

* * * * *

These persons vanished during daylight,
from different locations, on different dates,
and surrounded by other people.

Chapter 1
Thelma Pauline (Polly) Melton

Lot's wife was on Sodom and Gomorrah Road. She looked back and became a pillar of salt. Her fate is explained in the Bible.

On September 25, 1981, Polly Melton was hiking Deep Creek Trail in the Great Smoky Mountains National Park. She looked back and vanished. Her fate is yet to be explained.

Polly Melton, Trula Gudger, and Pauline (Red) Cannon were members of a group of about ten families who leased a campground beside Deep Creek in Swain County, North Carolina, and lived there in their travel trailers each summer.

The group did not admit any newcomers into their campground unless all the families voted unanimously to admit them. Most of them were retired, came in April or May, and stayed until October or November.

Weather permitting, Polly, Trula and Red hiked together each afternoon. When they met shortly after 3:00 PM on Friday, September 25, 1981, for a hike, the Airstream trailers sparkled under a bright sky. A few puffy clouds floated in a slight northeasterly breeze. The temperature was in the mid-80s. They decided to hike the Deep Creek Trail in the Great Smoky Mountains National Park, as they often

This is a view on Deep Creek Trail where Thelma
Pauline (Polly) Melton was last seen on
September 25, 1981.

This sign is at the entrance to Deep Creek Trail in the Great
Smoky Mountains National Park.

did. The trail is about four miles long, round trip. It begins near the private campground where they were camped, about a half-mile outside the Park. It ends about a mile and three-quarters into the Park. It is an excellent gravel road-bed which runs parallel to Deep Creek and is considered an easy trail.

Cars are permitted on Deep Creek Trail until the road splits about a quarter of a mile inside the Park. The right prong of the road provides access to a large picnic area and campground. The left prong is a continuation of Deep Creek Trail. About a hundred yards further, the trail narrows and there is a gate across it to keep out vehicular traffic. From this point on, tree and plant cover are very thick on each side of the trail.

As Polly, Red and Trula passed by the campground there were about fifty cars in the parking lot. Campers were setting up. A few hearty souls were swimming in Deep Creek, known for its cold water even in midsummer. Several horseback riders were in the area.

Polly Leaves Her Friends

Polly, Red and Trula reached the end of Deep Creek Trail, which everyone calls the turnaround, shortly before 4:00 PM. They paused briefly while Polly enjoyed a cigarette then began the hike back.

Having been friends for years, their intimate chatter was sprinkled with laughter. This day they each felt well and in good spirits, savoring the waning days of their 1981 camp-ground season.

They had hiked back about a half mile when, without explanation, Polly began to walk very fast, as if she intended to leave them behind. Trula and Red exchanged grins of amusement, thinking she would slow down. When she did not, Trula looked at Red. Red looked back at Trula. Mutual incomprehension.

Just as Polly was going out of earshot, Red called out, "I wouldn't want to be in a foot race with you, Polly."

Polly looked back, grinned impishly and chuckled as though satisfied with the situation. She picked up her pace and kept going. Trula and Red recall that her steps were quick and certain as she increased the distance between them. They saw her top over a hill and descend out of sight, still walking with a determined gait.

Anticipating Polly would tire quickly, they expected to overtake her. She would probably rest on a bench on the other side of the hill, where they usually stopped on the way back. Trula and Red continued hiking at their normal pace. They talked with the muted conviviality of persons who see each other every day, puzzling aloud occasionally about Polly's abrupt departure. When they topped over the hill, they were surprised not to see her sitting on the bench.

Just before Polly walked away, the trio had discussed Wilburn Surritte, whose wife had a trailer nearby. They laughed and joked that he must be taking time out from his "well known" habit of running around with other women because he had been at his wife's trailer twice during the past week.

Trula and Red had teased Polly about a 'handsome man' giving her the eye at the Bryson City Presbyterian Church Nutrition Center, where she did volunteer work serving meals to the elderly. They had laughed heartily and told Polly there was no use in denying it! Polly had not denied it but behaved as if watching herself so as not to do or say something wrong.

This was not out of the ordinary for Polly. She had friends but by and large kept her feelings to herself. Most of the time, she had a deliberation of movement and speech. On very rare occasions she would loosen up and banter a bit. Today, perhaps they had gone too far. Or had they unwittingly trampled into a very private part of Polly's life?

* * * * *

Polly had been married twice before she married Robert Melton at 52. She was now 58. Robert was now 78 and in very poor health. In her youth, Polly could probably have been described as an Amazonian beauty. She stood almost six feet, not heavy or fat, but an abundant Rubenesque type with golden auburn hair, placid face, and wide brown eyes.

Although she never confided that there had been lovers in her life, most of those who knew her best had little doubt. Polly was now overweight, suffered from high blood pressure and nausea, and took medication for them. She smoked over two packs of Virginia Slim cigarettes a day. Some of those who knew her had wondered privately if Polly was on the brink of domestic apocalypse. At times she seemed to be in the grip of depression, but not today.

Several hikers and joggers were on the trail, but it did not occur to Red or Trula to ask them about Polly.

They had no reason to be concerned for her safety. She had hiked this trail for almost 20 years. They had never known her to venture off it because of her very compelling fear of snakes. If they did not overtake her on the trail, they expected to find her back at her Airstream trailer.

Neither had an inkling that Thelma Pauline (Polly) Melton had vanished.

Discovering Polly Had Vanished

Trula and Red arrived at their campground about 4:30 PM and headed for the Meltons' Airstream. They would ascertain that she had returned, iron out any prickly feelings and go to their respective trailers to rest before the evening meal.

They had no thought of anything but an amicable, routine evening as the evenings had been for years within this tightly-knitted circle of campers. They enjoyed being together.

Bob Melton was alone in the Airstream. They told him what had happened, then walked around the campground quickly, asking everyone in sight if they had seen Polly. No one had. They were becoming concerned, but not alarmed, and hoped she would walk into view so they could tell her what she had put them through.

Red located her husband, Jack Cannon, and told him what had happened. Trula went to Avis Love's trailer and told her because she and Polly were friends. The four of them searched their private campground, the Deep Creek Campground and picnic area within the Park.

One possibility was that Polly had met someone she knew on the part of the trail where automobiles are permitted and accepted a ride. Bob Melton and her fellow campers were confident she would never have gotten into an automobile with anyone she did not know unless she was forced to do so. Polly did not know many people outside their campground with whom she would accept a ride. It was decided Bob Melton and Avis Love would call everyone they could think of and ask if they had seen Polly or had given her a ride.

Trula, Red and Jack Cannon would hike to the spot on Deep Creek Trail where Polly was last seen. They asked everyone on the trail if they had seen Polly. No one had. There were no obvious signs on either side of the trail of anyone having left it.

The three returned to their campground jumpy as fleas. Avis Love met them with a shake of her head.

Time to Get Help

They were convinced Polly was not on Deep Creek Trail. Instinctively they looked at Deep Creek. Deep Creek is a dippy, bouncing creek, noisy as a freeway as the water flows through a narrow channel around boulders and over rocks. Polly was habitually cautious about the creek.

The sky was still bright; but the Smoky Mountains would be wrapped in darkness within a short time, and the night would be chilly. It was time to report Polly's disappearance. At 6:00 PM on September 25, 1981, Avis Love filed a report with Park ranger Dennis Burnett that Thelma Pauline Melton had been missing since about 4:00 PM.

Thelma Pauline (Polly) Melton

Age: 58

Sex: Female

Race: Caucasian

Height: 5' 10"

Weight:

170 - 180 pounds

Hair: auburn,

shoulder length

Eyes: brown, wearing glasses with heavy, dark brown frames

Physical condition: suffers from high blood pressure and nausea, takes medication for these ailments

Clothing: white and pink striped sleeveless blouse and tan polyester pants

Shoes: tan, low cut, size 8 1/2, with crepe soles, which would leave a distinctive footprint because the left shoe sole had a crack across the ball of the foot

Personal items: Virginia Slim cigarettes, a diamond-studded white gold wrist watch and wedding band

Ranger Burnett called other rangers, most of whom knew her. Not one of them had seen Polly after 4:00 PM. He searched for an hour, then called for help.

What Had Happened That Day?

Ranger Burnett wanted as much detail as possible about what Polly Melton had done during the day before she went missing. Had anyone noticed anything unusual? This line of inquiry was made with the hope it would provide leads to follow if she was not found. Her friends and husband supplied as much information as they could recall.

Except for walking away rapidly, without explanation, on Deep Creek Trail, Polly Melton's behavior had seemed normal to Red and Trula. It had also seemed normal to her husband Bob Melton.

She had followed her daily routine, except she had not gone to the Nutrition Center to serve meals to the elderly as she usually did on Friday. She did not explain why to anyone; but this was volunteer work, and she was free to set her own schedule. No one thought it might be important until she disappeared.

Prior to hiking with Red and Trula, Polly had prepared sauce for the spaghetti she intended to cook for supper, and taken a short nap.

If she took money, identification, or medicine with her, these items had been concealed from Red and Trula. Polly was barred from driving an automobile that summer, so she had no car keys and no keys to their trailer since Bob was there.

Polly's Family

The Meltons were from Jacksonville, Florida. They rented space there for their Airstream trailer, which was their full-time home. They also rented a shed to store the few items they owned that would not fit in the trailer. They planned to return to Jacksonville for the winter, but no definite departure date had been set.

Polly had no children. Bob Melton had two sons, who appeared to keep Polly at a distance. When one of her stepsons was notified she was missing, he said his only interest was the impact on his father.

Polly became very close to her father, Fred H. McAllister, Sr., after her mother died in 1978. He had come from his home in Leeds, Alabama, about the middle of September and visited with her. When he was contacted the first evening she was missing, he said she had not seemed troubled and had no reason to think she would leave of her own free will.

Kit Postell, Polly's only and younger sister, and her husband Jim, lived in Charlotte, North Carolina. Bob Melton called them shortly after Polly went missing. They had no reason to believe Polly would leave without telling anyone and became very concerned for her safety.

Kit Postell contacted their four brothers. Neither brother could entertain the notion of Polly willingly walking away from the life she was leading.

The consensus among them was that if she wanted to leave she would tell her husband and family, just as she had when her other two marriages had ended. Despite the conviction of family and friends, persons who deliberately go missing are not really uncommon. Therefore, this possibility could not be discounted. However, there were no immediate leads in that direction to follow. Consequently a search for Polly Melton was conducted.

Initial Search

Ranger Burnett closed Deep Creek Trail to the public. Within a short time, 25 persons, Park rangers and civilian volunteers, had assembled to search for Polly Melton. After he briefed them, an intensive search of Deep Creek Trail, and all the side trails Polly might have taken, was completed by dusk.

The side trails were Noland Divide, Indian Creek and Hammer Branch Trail to Juneywhank Falls.

Rangers and volunteers questioned each person coming off Deep Creek Trail during the night. No one had seen Polly Melton or anything unusual.

As the word spread, more volunteers joined in the search. After dark, some of the searchers concentrated on Deep Creek, shining bright lights into the water. Others walked the trails, but there was no trace of Polly.

The evening crept edgily on. Bob Melton became distraught as the reports came in that there were no clues to Polly's whereabouts. He was admitted to the Swain County Hospital before midnight.

Jim Postell, Polly's brother-in-law, was especially concerned that she had met with foul play. He told Ranger

Burnett that he knew there was a drug drop called Poke Patch where addicts hung out. He believed it was close to where Polly was last seen. His fear was that a drug addict had seen the white gold wristwatch and wedding band Polly was wearing and kidnapped her to rob her.

Poke Patch is over four miles from where Polly Melton was last seen. Considering her physical condition, fear of snakes, and the rough terrain, this possibility seemed highly unlikely. She would have probably collapsed if forced to walk under duress.

Polly's weight, 170 -180 pounds, would be a heavy load for anyone to carry very far in any direction. It would be almost impossible to carry her through the deep thickets that border Deep Creek Trail. Anyone capable of carrying Polly Melton, or forcing her to walk against her will, would have been almost certain to have attracted the attention of the many campers, horseback riders and fishermen in and around Deep Creek that afternoon.

The authorities determined Poke Patch would be searched, but the territory surrounding Deep Creek Trail where she was last seen would be searched first.

* * * * *

Polly's father and two of her brothers arrived about 9:00 PM to join in the search. Authorities hoped they could provide additional information, but they had talked among themselves on the way and had no ideas. They feared she had been kidnapped or injured by a drug addict who had robbed her.

The night of September 25, 1981, was clear and dry, and the temperature dropped into the low 50s. Polly Melton, in her sleeveless blouse and lightweight pants, would have been uncomfortable but in no danger of getting wet or freezing.

There had been no rain for over a week. That would make it difficult for her to find water unless she was close to Deep Creek. Assuming she did not suffer an attack of nausea or complications from her high blood pressure, those experienced in such matters believed she could survive the night.

Media Coverage

Local media coverage was immediate and intensive. Requests for anyone with information about Polly Melton to contact the Park Service were made frequently on the local radio and television stations. Few leads came in, and none were worthwhile. However, several volunteers called offering to help search.

Within twenty-four hours, the story was in newspapers and on radio and television nationwide. A few reporters came to the search site, but most relied on Park Service press releases. No news organization kept a reporter at the scene. The family furnished photographs of Polly, and they were distributed to newspapers and television stations in cities on the East Coast.

The Official Park Service Search

The search for Thelma Pauline Melton is one of the shortest searches ever made in the Great Smoky Mountains for a person who vanished without a trace. It began about 7:00 PM on Friday, September 25, 1981, approximately three hours after she was last seen, and ended one week later, October 2, 1981.

During the week, approximately 150 persons, 9 dogs and their handlers, 5 or 6 friends, and 3 family members searched for Polly.

The dry weather made it almost impossible for dogs to track Polly Melton. One bloodhound, Missy, kept returning to a downed tree beside Deep Creek Trail. Persons sit on the tree to rest. Bob Swabe, Missy's handler, concluded Polly Melton had been at this spot, but Missy could not pick up her trail away from it. All the other dog handlers turned in totally negative reports.

* * * * *

Thelma Pauline (Polly) Melton's disappearance was entered into the National Criminal Information Center computer on Saturday, September 26, 1981.

* * * * *

Deep Creek Trail was reopened on Tuesday, September 29, 1981. Word was passed to those using it to be on the lookout for Polly. No one reported anything.

The Search Ends

Officials of the Great Smoky Mountains National Park told the press on October 2, 1981, that the evidence indicated Polly Melton had left the Park, probably in an automobile of her own free will.

With so many persons in the area at the time she disappeared, they believed a departure under duress would probably have been noticed and reported. Therefore, it was reasonable to conclude the dogs would have picked up her scent, whether dead or alive, if she had still been in the Park.

No motive for or evidence of foul play had been found, and neither has been found.

Analyzing Polly's Life

As with any disappearance, the life of Thelma Pauline Melton was scrutinized by the authorities for possible leads.

Polly attended Victory Baptist Church on Deep Creek frequently, but was not a member, On Monday, September 28, 1981, following Polly's disappearance on Friday, Tom Harris, Pastor of Victory Baptist Church, told Park rangers Mrs. Melton had spoken with him and seemed slightly depressed of late. But, he emphasized, not as depressed as she had been two years ago when she was a heavy user of valium. In his opinion, she was not suicidal but was not as active or tidy as she had been in the spring.

Apparently from a contact with Bob Melton, Pastor Harris had found out that a bottle of valium prescribed for Bob Melton was missing from their trailer. Bob missed it after Polly disappeared.

Pastor Harris thought one conversation with Mrs. Melton might be significant. It had occurred about three years before she disappeared. Her mother had just died, and she was still grieving. He had tried to comfort her with the thought she would see her mother in heaven one day. Mrs. Melton had said she wanted to go to heaven and had then talked about persons who were 'running around' on their spouses. She said she would never do that

In thinking back over the conversation, Pastor Harris said he had come to feel that Mrs. Melton had committed adultery and felt guilty.

Pastor Harris declined to furnish any more specifics of his conversations with Mrs. Melton. In sum, his information supported the confidential observations made to Park rangers by a few of her fellow campers but offered nothing concrete to investigate.

* * * * *

Contacts with Polly Melton's two former husbands and coworkers yielded no leads.

Her first husband was a career Army man, and they had traveled many places together. Her second husband was an MIT graduate who worked at Howard University in Washington, DC.

Polly had worked for Sears, the federal government, and taught school in Alaska.

* * * * *

On October 6, 1981, Nell Rickman, the supervisor at the Bryson City Presbyterian Church Nutrition Center, provided the authorities with new information. She had been away when Mrs. Melton disappeared, and this caused the delay in reporting what she knew.

The procedure at the Center was for volunteers to sign up at the end of the day for the next day they intended to work. Mrs. Melton worked on Thursday, September 24,

1981, but did not sign up to work on Friday, September 25, 1981. She did not offer any explanation, although she usually worked on Friday. If she could not be there, she usually said why.

In addition to not signing up for Friday, Mrs. Melton did something else unusual for her. For the first time in all the years she had worked at the Center, she asked to use the church telephone several times on Thursday, September 24, 1981.

Mrs. Rickman did not hear her conversations. There were no long distance charges on the telephone. Investigators were not able to determine the numbers she had called. No family member or friend remembers her calling them on September 24, 1981.

Several of the patrons at the Center told Juanitta Baldwin that they found Mrs. Melton friendly and helpful. All of them were genuinely puzzled at her disappearance.

Once Polly had joked with them about her weight, declaring she had lost her commitment to a lemon juice and salad diet somewhere in the twelfth hour and never intended to try that again.

After Mrs. Melton disappeared someone remembered a conversation about fate and wishes coming true. She had joined in the laughter about some of the far-out wishes.

Mrs. Melton was asked what she would wish for. She smiled for a moment, then quipped, "If Fate would grant me a wish, I would wish to be light enough to walk without leaving footprints."

After the Park Service Search Ended

Kit Postell contacted the Sheriff of Swain County, North Carolina, the North Carolina Bureau of Investigation and the Federal Bureau of Investigation. Each agency told her this disappearance was not within their jurisdiction. They would, however, report any lead that came to their attention to the proper authorities.

* * * * *

Bob Melton returned to Florida as soon as he was released from the Swain County Hospital. A year later, with the help of his sons, he returned to Deep Creek and sold their Airstream trailer and station wagon, severing ties to their summer home.

Shortly after this trip, Bob Melton was admitted to a nursing home in Gainesville, Florida, suffering from heart trouble and emphysema. His sons have refused to discuss the disappearance of their stepmother, Polly Melton, with media representatives.

* * * * *

In December 1981, friends of Kit Postell sent a petition with 200 signatures to the governor of North Carolina, James Hunt, asking for help. In November 1983, Governor Hunt announced a reward of $5,000 for information to help locate Thelma Pauline Melton.

It has never been claimed.

James G. Martin, Mrs. Postell's congressman, wrote to the Department of Interior on her behalf. The response he received on February 5, 1982, was that the case was still open and each lead that came in had been checked and would continue to be checked.

* * * * *

In March 1982, a National Guard helicopter flew down the Deep Creek drainage area. The heavy foliage had made it impossible to see the ground from the air in September when Polly disappeared.

The flight took place on a day with good visibility and little wind so low flying was possible. The trees were bare, but nothing was spotted.

Deep Creek is a favorite spot for tubing - the sport of floating along in an inflated innertube. When the water is high, hundreds of persons tube and picnic on the banks. Fishing in Deep Creek is almost a ritual for many locals and tourists. No one engaging in these activities has reported a clue relating to Polly Melton.

Did Polly Melton Cash a Check in 1982?

After Polly disappeared on September 25, 1981, investigators checked her only known private bank account at the Atlantic Bank, Lake Forest Branch, in Jacksonville, Florida. There had been no unusual transactions. The last transaction was on September 15, 1981.

On April 14, 1982, a check made payable to Pauline Melton, drawn on the Birmingham Trust National Bank of Birmingham, Alabama, was cashed.

The check represented the interest due on a bank certificate. The signature on the check appeared to be Pauline Melton's. The Great Smoky Mountains National Park officials learned about this check. They attempted to determine if Mrs. Melton was alive and well and had cashed the check or if another individual had forged her signature for purposes of financial gain.

The bank checked into the matter. The teller who had cashed the check could not remember the person who had cashed it. The expense of employing handwriting experts was prohibitive in the absence of any other evidence which might help locate Polly Melton.

Did Polly Melton Walk Away?

Case #813356 on Thelma Pauline (Polly) Melton is still open in 2009.

There have been rumors that she simply walked away from her life and began a new life with a new partner. Numerous reports that she has been seen in Florida, and in other states, have been received since she disappeared.

Each time a report has been checked, it has come to a dead end. Her body has not been found.

This is one of few cases where Park officials have not received offers of help from psychics.

While researching this book, Juanitta Baldwin spoke with several Park rangers who knew Polly Melton during the 20 years she had camped at Deep Creek. All of them are convinced she was too intelligent and too strong to have gone with a kidnapper without a struggle. They remember her as a big woman and a pleasant camper who knew the area too well to have become lost, even under medication. They believe she would have simply sat down or would have had to lie down, and she would have been found.

The rangers said there was no bear or other animal in the area large enough to have eaten or dragged away a woman her size so fast that no trace of her could be found by the time the search was made.

Avis Love's Observations

Avis Love, Polly's friend and fellow camper who reported her missing on September 25, 1981 was 80 years old when Juanitta Baldwin spoke with her. She was still spending her summers in her trailer, which is parked in the same private campground beside Deep Creek where she and Polly were camped when Polly disappeared.

She has never heard from Polly and has no idea what could have happened to her. Through the years, she has heard numerous rumors but does not have any reason to believe any of them are true. Having lived so long, Avis Love is certain that no one vanishes into thin air. All she knows is that Polly Melton went somewhere, and she hopes to know where she went while she still lives.

Will Polly's Fate Ever Be Known?

As said at the beginning of this story, Lot's wife looked back and became a pillar of salt. Her fate is explained in the Bible. Polly looked back and vanished. Perhaps Fate granted her wish to walk without leaving footprints.

Chapter 2
Trenny Lynn Gibson

Trenny Lynn Gibson, 16, disappeared on October 8, 1976. She vanished without a trace on the trail between Andrews Bald and the Clingmans Dome parking area in the Great Smoky Mountains National Park.

* * * * *

Trenny Gibson, a junior at Bearden High School in Knoxville, Tennessee, was excited about going on a horticultural field trip on Friday, October 8, 1976. Her mother, Hope Gibson, recalls Trenny thought the school officials might cancel the trip because the weather forecast was for rain and cooler temperatures. She suggested Trenny dress warmly because of the weather forecast, and the fact that the trip supervisor had not told them where they were going.

Trenny left home wearing blue jeans, a blue blouse, a blue and white striped sweater, blue Adidas shoes, a star sapphire and diamond ring but did not take a jacket nor hat. Later in the day, she borrowed a brown plaid jacket from Robert Simpson.

Hope drove Trenny to school. She asked a student passing by if the field trip was on and was told it was a go.

Trenny took her lunch but left her books and pocket-book in her mother's car so she had no identification nor money with her that day. She kissed her mother good-bye and joined other students on the sidewalk.

Trenny Lynn Gibson

This photograph was taken on October 7, 1976, the day before she vanished in the Great Smoky Mountains National Park.

Hope Gibson waved and drove away, anticipating seeing Trenny after the trip.

Wayne Dunlap, a teacher, was the only person supervising the field trip. The 40 students were enthused and boarded the bus in a state of high anticipation. Mr. Dunlap announced they were headed for the Great Smoky Mountains National Park and was rewarded with whistles, cheers and applause.

He explained the itinerary for the trip. The bus would park in the Clingmans Dome parking area. They would hike the trail to Andrews Bald and return to the bus on the same trail. Although Andrews Bald is close to Clingmans Dome, a mountain with an observation tower at its peak, no one was to go further than Andrews Bald or take any side trails. Their assignment during the hike was to observe the trees and plants but not to break any plant or gather anything.

Everyone was to be back at the bus by 3:30 PM. After a show of hands that his instructions were clear, the students were left to enjoy the trip.

Trenny shared a seat with Robert Simpson. They laughed and joked between themselves and with other students during the trip, which took about two hours.

The bus arrived at the Clingmans Dome parking area around 12:30 PM. The skies were overcast, and it was chilly. Wayne Dunlap reminded everyone to take their coats or jackets and to be back at the bus by 3:30 PM. Within minutes the students were on their way to Andrews Bald, laughing, talking and yelling.

A few students challenged each other to a race to Andrews Bald and left the majority behind. They broke into smaller groups suited to their hiking pace.

Trenny and Robert Simpson hiked to Andrews Bald together. When most of the students decided to begin the hike back, Trenny went with them. Robert stayed behind.

The hike to Andrews Bald and back to the bus was expected to be accomplished in about three hours. It appeared to be a routine field trip. The students hiked, socialized, ate the lunches they had brought with them, and generally had a good time.

No one seemed intent on studying the plants and trees, especially after the rain began to move in. The temperature was dropping, and some students were not dressed warmly enough. They ran and jumped about to keep warm.

Trenny Disappears

By 3:30 PM all the students, except Trenny Gibson, were ready to board the bus. Wayne Dunlap questioned them and established that Trenny had left Andrews Bald with a small group about 2:00 PM.

Bobbie Coghill said, "I was walking with Angela Beckner and Lisa Mikels when Trenny came up behind us. Trenny was walking faster than us, so I started walking with her.

"We caught up with Scott Troy and Anita Rounds. We walked with them for about five minutes. I asked if anybody else was breathing hard, and Trenny said, 'Yeah, everybody!' Then somebody said, 'Let's rest,' and everybody stopped and sat down but Trenny. She said she did not want to stop and kept going."

Anita Rounds said, "We were about a half or three-quarters of a mile from the Clingman's Dome parking area when Trenny left us. We were watching her, and it looked as if she turned right off the trail. David Easteman came up from behind, and I looked at him. When I looked back down the trail Trenny was not there. We thought she would be at the bus."

The students had left Andrews Bald in small groups. There were several groups ahead of and several groups behind Trenny's group. According to their statements, no student saw Trenny after she walked away alone on the trail about 3:00 PM.

* * * * *

Robert Simpson had spent more time on the trip with Trenny than anyone else. The next day he was asked to write down everything he could remember about the day Trenny disappeared. This is what he wrote.

Otober 9, 1976

On the way up to the mountains, I sat with Trenny and we would crack a few jokes, and she seemed to be in a good mood. When we got to the trail going to Andrews Bald, we sat down and ate. I don't think she was meaning to take off anywhere because she gave me part of her sandwich.

When I started down the trail to Andrews Bald, I asked her if she was going to come with me, then she started down the trail. We hiked about a mile, then stopped for a rest, she was breathing kind of hard so we sat down for about five minutes. When we reached the Andrews Bald, she was still in good spirits, so we looked around a little bit then got under a tree when it started raining.

By the time everyone else got there, she was rested up and ready to start back. She asked me if I was coming with the group back to the bus and I said I was going to stay a little longer.

She said good-by and that was the last I saw of her. When I got back to the bus I saw that she was gone and so did some of the others, so we started asking some of the people that she was with and they said that they stopped to rest but she kept on going, plus they said that the trail went to the left but she went to the right and nobody has seen her since.

The last time I saw Trenny I was at Andrews Bald. We reached the Bald at about 1:30.

* * * * *

At 3:40 PM Trenny had not come to the bus. Wayne Dunlap and Danny Johnson, a student, began a search for Trenny. Wayne admonished the other students to look around the parking area but to remain in it. Danny hiked to Andrews Bald but found nothing. Wayne searched the nearby trail to Double Springs.

Trenny still had not appeared by the time Wayne and Danny returned. The students reported they had looked all over the parking area and questioned most of the people in the parking area. No one had any information about Trenny.

Trenny is Reported Missing

At 4:06 PM, Wayne Dunlap contacted the National Park Service by CB radio. Park Ranger Sammy Lail responded and arrived at the Clingmans Dome parking area at 4:30 PM. Wayne told him what had happened and where they had searched.

After he made a search of the Andrews Bald area, Ranger Lail made an official report that Trenny Lynn Gibson was missing in the Great Smoky Mountains National Park.

The Park Service launched a search for Trenny Gibson as soon as Ranger Lail's report was received. Park personnel and rescue squad personnel in nearby areas of Tennessee and North Carolina were requested to help.

* * * * *

Shortly after 5:00 PM, the students boarded their bus to return to Knoxville. Wayne Dunlap stayed behind to help with the search. He told Ranger Lail that the consensus among the departing students was more interest than alarm, and it was generally thought that Trenny had run off with someone. Wayne did not share their opinion, but he could not shed any light on what had happened to her.

By this time, strong winds were buffeting the mountains with heavy rain; and the temperature was in the low 30s. Despite the raw weather, several groups of searchers responded. A total of 19 arrived between 6:30 and 8:00 PM. Although hampered by the wind, rain and fog, the groups fanned out and began combing the area where the students had hiked, especially where Trenny was last seen.

All search reports were coming in negative. No group could find any clue to follow.

Trenny's Parents are Notified

After the students returned to Bearden High School around 7:30 PM, the principal, Frank Hall, was notified. Between 8:00 and 8:30 PM, Hope Gibson received a telephone call which she would later describe this way.

"Talmage Hooker, a guidance counselor from Bearden High School, called. He said, 'Trenny has been lost in the mountains.' After he did not hear a reply, he said, 'I guess you are in shock.'"

"The school officials had known Trenny was missing for over five hours before they called me. Further, the school authorities did not inform the parents of the destination of the field trip in advance or secure permission from the parents. Had we known, we could have refused to allow Trenny to go on that trip to the mountains when the weather was so threatening."

Robert J. Gibson, Sr., Trenny's father, was in New Orleans on business. He was due to arrive at the Knoxville airport at 9:30 PM. Mr. Talmage Hooker, who had notified Hope that Trenny was lost, accompanied her to the airport. Mr. Gibson's flight was on time. After he was told that Trenny was missing in the Great Smoky Mountains National Park and that a search was underway, he called the Park Headquarters. Trenny had not been found.

He informed them that he and Mrs. Gibson would come to the area as soon as possible. The search officials requested him to bring clothing which Trenny had worn so it could be used to give scent to the search dogs which would be used if Trenny was not found during the night.

They drove to Park Headquarters, arriving around midnight. Search officials briefed them on the search, which was still being hampered by heavy rain, wind, temperatures in the 30s, and dense fog. At 3:00 AM, the search was suspended until the next morning.

The Gibsons checked into the River Terrace Motel in nearby Gatlinburg. The owners were concerned and provided them rooms free of charge for five days.

A Full-Scale Search Begins

A full-scale search for Trenny began on October 9, 1976, with Park Ranger Jack Linahan as the coordinator. He closed the road between Clingmans Dome parking area and Newfound Gap to the public.

Personnel began assembling in the Clingmans Dome parking area shortly before 7:00 AM. Four dog handlers with well-trained German shepherds and bloodhounds arrived.

The rain had tapered off during the night, and the temperature had dropped below freezing. Strong winds howled across the mountains bringing heavy cloud cover and thick fog. Visibility was almost zero.

The searchers had to be screened to ascertain they were physically fit and sufficiently trained to go into the rugged mountains, search, and come out without injury. Even with these precautions, several searchers were injured during the search for Trenny; but there was no loss of life.

Dr. Robert Lash and his medical team from the University of Tennessee came and set up operations. They were on standby during the entire search and treated the injured.

Food and drink for the searchers was a monumental problem. On the first morning of the search, a Red Cross unit arrived with a portable food wagon that served hot and cold drinks, donuts and pastries.

By noon, the local restaurants had heard the news and brought food, drinks and snacks.

Between the Red Cross and the local restaurants and other concerned merchants, there was always an ample supply of food throughout the search. All of this was provided free of charge.

* * * * *

After the searchers were screened, Ranger Linahan briefed them and assigned groups to various grids in the area from Clingmans Dome parking area to Andrews Bald and all side trails.

The Gibsons had brought clothing that Trenny had worn, and they watched hopefully as the bloodhounds and German shepherds took up the scent. Although the area where Anita Rounds thought she saw Trenny go to the right of the trail had already been searched twice the night before it was thoroughly searched again. The dogs could not pick up any scent.

There is no side trail at that point on the trail. The terrain is rocky; the ground is very rough and is overgrown with trees and thick underbrush and briars. A small stream makes the bank slick. A few ferns close to the trail were broken but there was nothing to indicate Trenny had left the trail at this point.

The searchers found three wet cigarette butts and a beer can with some beer in it still fresh enough to smell close to the spot where Trenny was last seen. It was established that Trenny did not smoke. No student was known to have brought beer to the Park the day of the hike to Andrews Bald.

* * * * *

Several National Guard helicopters had been obtained for the search, but it was late afternoon before the fog lifted enough for them to fly. Even then, the haze, thick evergreen foliage and turning leaves on other vegetation made it almost impossible to see anything on the ground.

The temperature rose only into the 40s where there was sunlight. The humidity was high and searchers became exhausted quickly. The call for help was extended over a wider area. Reinforcements arrived all day to relieve those too tired to continue.

All morning the search reports were negative. No sign, no track, no tangible clue had been found.

Media

Hope and Robert Gibson walked some of the trails until reporters from newspapers and television stations arrived.

They appealed to them to publicize Trenny's disappearance so anyone who had seen her or anything that could help find her might come forward.

Both pleaded with the reporters to write their stories so everyone would understand that coming forward with information might save their daughter's life.

They furnished photographs of Trenny - one with her poodle, Mitzi, who slept with her every night. Trenny was described as being 5' 3" tall, 115 pounds, green eyes, long, straight brown hair, pierced ears, right-handed, and not wearing glasses. Her parents considered her levelheaded and not likely to panic, although she is not experienced in the mountains. They emphasized that Trenny was with several boys, mostly at school, but was not dating anyone at the time. She did not have a driver's license.

The Gibsons have three other children. Robert Gibson, Jr., 19 and in the Navy, Tina 14, and Miracle 5. Hope Gibson told reporters that she and Robert are close to their children, and the children are close to each other.

Tremendous media coverage began on October 9, 1976; and there were follow-up stories each day until the search ended. The Park Service issued an all-points bulletin to hospitals and law enforcement agencies.

End of the First Day of Searching

At the end of the day, all the reports were negative. It was as if Trenny Gibson had vanished into thin air.

At sundown, Ranger Linahan met with the Gibsons and told them everything that had been done that day. Several of the dogs had tracked Trenny to a spot on the paved road about 1.6 miles from the Clingmans Dome parking area. He explained this could mean Trenny had reached this road, unseen by anyone in her student group. She could have left the Park from that road, possibly in a vehicle.

Possibly, the Gibsons conceded; but they were firm in their conviction that if Trenny had left the Park, it would have been against her will. They completely rejected the suggestion made by some of her fellow students that Trenny had planned to run away or had run away on the spur of the moment. If she had planned to run away, she was smart enough to prepare.

The Gibsons explained their reasons for believing Trenny had not planned on leaving the Park during the school trip to Ranger Linahan and the media.

She left over $200 cash in her room, and she had not taken any money from her savings account.

She had injured her foot about three weeks prior to her disappearance and was still taking medicine for it. She left the medicine at home.

She was looking forward to spending time over the weekend with her brother Robert Jr., home on leave from the Navy. Robert and Hope Gibson emphasized they did not want their rejection of the idea of Trenny running away to lessen the search for her outside the Park. They wanted persons to be very alert to signs of a young girl in danger or being held against her will. Robert Gibson went on radio to ask for prayers that their daughter might be returned safely.

Trenny's Chances of Survival

Search officials believed that if Trenny managed to keep dry she might be able to survive for as long as a week since she was wearing fairly warm clothing.

If she had reached the spot on the road where the dogs stopped, the possibility remained that she could still be in the Park; and the full-scale search would be resumed at daybreak the next day.

The Third Day of the Search

On Sunday, October 10, 1976, there were over 300 volunteer searchers, about 30 park rangers, and three Tennessee Air National Guard helicopters ready to resume the search for Trenny.

It was very foggy, but the rain had moved out during the night. Gradually the fog lifted; the afternoon was sunny and in the upper 40s, and a few flights were made. Abundant hoarfrost was frozen to the trees on the shady side of the mountains which reflected the sunlight and made the already difficult visibility situation worse.

At various times on Sunday, three different dogs tracked to the same location where the dogs had tracked Trenny to on Saturday.

The searchers also found eight cigarette butts at this spot. The cigarette butts were the same brand as the three butts found at the point on Andrews Bald trail where Trenny was last seen.

* * * * *

At the end of the day on Sunday, David Bossard, Western North Carolina Rescue Squad leader, told a reporter from *The Asheville Citizen,* "This intensive search would have found her if she is in the Park. Let's face it. It was below freezing with a 15 mile an hour wind that put it about zero. If she stayed in the Park, I don't think she could be alive. The officials think she got a ride out of the Park, or teamed up with some hikers on the Appalachian Trail, and was never lost."

Park officials conceded the validity of his remarks but assured the Gibsons the full-scale search would continue at daybreak on Monday, October 11, 1976.

Fears About Abduction or Foul Play

The Park Service believed that tracking what was believed to be Trenny's trail to the road, and finding the beer can and cigarette butts increased the possibility of abduction or foul play.

The Gibsons were worried about foul play. They told Ranger Linahan about an event which had resulted in public threats being made to kill Trenny. At first they declined to give specifics, but said they feared the person who had made the threats had somehow 'gotten to' Trenny up there in the wilderness.

The FBI Enters the Case

The Park Service requested the FBI to investigate the disappearance of Trenny Gibson. On Tuesday, October 12, 1976, the fourth day after Trenny disappeared, the FBI entered the case. If she had been kidnapped in the Park, it would be under their jurisdiction.

Special Agent Harold C. Swanson, based in the Knoxville, Tennessee, office of the FBI, told the press that they had no evidence that Trenny had been kidnapped; but they were working on two theories.

The primary theory was that Trenny was abducted at the point where the Andrews Bald Trail intersects with the Appalachian Trail. She could then have been taken to the fog-shrouded tower on Clingman Dome by her captor(s) and hidden until it was safe to walk unseen to the spot on the road to which she was tracked by the dogs. From there, she could have been whisked out of the Park.

The secondary theory was that when Trenny walked alone ahead of her classmates, she somehow became lost in the rain and fog. She might have followed the Appalachian Trail by mistake and made her way to the tower at Clingmans Dome. From there she could possibly have seen automobile lights and made her way to the road. Instead of the help she was probably looking for, she was abducted or met with some other kind of foul play.

A thorough investigation was conducted, but no evidence has ever been found to substantiate either theory or to develop any new theories.

The Threats Against Trenny

Specific details of the incident which had resulted in alleged threats against Trenny came to light a few days later when Robert and Hope Gibson and their 14 year old daughter, Tina, came to see Ranger Linahan.

Several students had told Mr. Gibson that they had seen Kelvin Bowman following the bus on the way to the Clingmans Dome parking area. They also told him that

Trenny's hair comb had ended up in Robert Simpson's car. He said he had asked the Knox County Sheriff to check out the young man, Kelvin Bowman, who had made the threats against Trenny and to find out how Trenny's comb got in Robert Simpson's car.

Mr. Gibson said his fear that Kelvin Bowman might be involved had also been heightened by statements Robert Simpson, the classmate who had hiked to Andrews Bald with Trenny, had made to Tina.

Tina said Robert Simpson had visited the Gibson residence twice while her parents were staying at the motel in Gatlinburg right after Trenny disappeared. During these visits, Tina quoted him as saying, "If Kelvin Bowman has Trenny, he will kill her. If he does not have her, I think she might have run off with some horny hitchhiker."

The Gibsons said Kelvin Bowman had been trying to date Trenny about two years prior. He and another young man, Ronnie Joiner, had come to the Gibson residence late at night. Kelvin Bowman had broken into Trenny's bedroom. Hope Gibson shot Bowman in the foot, and the police were called.

Kelvin Bowman had been arrested and tried. He was sentenced to a correctional institution. While in the courtroom, he had allegedly made threats to kill Trenny when he got out.

The Knox County Sheriff's Department investigated any possible involvement by Kelvin Bowman. Wayne Dunlap, the teacher who was on the bus supervising the field trip, was adamant that no cars followed the bus. He could be so positive, he said, because no one had been told where they were going until the bus had departed the school grounds.

Mr. Frank Hall, Bearden High Principal, stated that Kelvin Bowman was in school on Friday, October 8, 1976, the day Trenny disappeared. This was verified by other sources, and Kelvin Bowman was quickly cleared of any suspicion in Trenny's disappearance.

* * * * *

There is no record that the report to Robert Gibson by Trenny's classmates that her comb was found in Robert Simpson's car was investigated.

Public Relations

In addition to the monumental logistical problems of conducting such a large, intensive search, the Park Service was required to spend much time with the media and the public. Media coverage was considered an essential component of the search, and there were daily press briefings. As the days passed, fewer reporters came to the scene. Press releases were issued to reach as many people as possible, with the hope someone would recognize Trenny.

Many persons who claimed to be psychic, or who had dreamed where Trenny could be found, called to volunteer their help. Each call was recorded and checked out. The following calls are typical of the hundreds received during the search for Trenny.

Telephone Calls

Cecil Thomas in Nashville, Tennessee, called on October 13, 1976. He said he was a psychic and had experienced a vision that Trenny was still alive or else was frozen in a sitting position, just a little to the left of the area they were searching at the time of his call.

"I saw her near the mouth of a creek, sitting in a hollow in what might be a bear den or something - rocky area - not a lot of undergrowth - several very old, large trees - sun shining directly down through a light layer of fog - lots of squirrels running around eating acorns. There are many acorns on the ground in the area."

* * * * *

An anonymous call was made by a male to the Knoxville, Tennessee, Police Department. The caller told the dispatcher that Trenny had been raped and stabbed. The caller said her body could be found at a point where Abrams Creek and the West Prong meet.

Both of these streams are in the Park, but they are miles apart and do not meet at any point.

* * * * *

Mrs. Louise Linderman of Maryville, Tennessee, called on October 22, 1976, to say she had been having dreams about Trenny Gibson. She 'felt' Trenny was still in the Park and was under a tree - possibly a hickory, on a down slope exposed to the afternoon sun - and was within five miles of where she disappeared. She was not sure if Trenny would be found there dead or alive.

Sightings Reported During the Search

Dozens of calls were received that Trenny had been seen in various locations in North Carolina and Tennessee. A call from Mrs. Elmer Huskey, who lived on Chapman Highway in Knoxville, sparked great hope for a short time. Mrs. Huskey reported that a girl who looked like the pictures she had seen of Trenny Gibson had come to her home between 7:00 and 8:00 PM on October 22, 1976. The girl asked if she could use her telephone to ask for help because she and her friends were having car trouble. Mrs. Huskey said she allowed the girl to use her telephone to make a collect call but got no answer. She did not know who she called.

The girl then went across the street to the residence of Mr. and Mrs. Woodrow Shuler and asked if anyone could help her and her friends with their car trouble. When they informed the girl they could not, she got into a car with several other young people, and they drove away. Neither Mrs. Huskey nor the Shulers asked the girl her name or where she lived.

The Shulers also believed the girl was Trenny Gibson and recorded the make and license number of the car in which she was riding. They went to Park Headquarters the next day with this information. They were shown photographs of Trenny and positively identified her as the girl who had come to their home.

The information was forwarded to the FBI. They located the registered owner of the car immediately. The young girl was identified, and she verified she had been at the Huskey and Shuler homes asking for help. She was not Trenny Gibson.

* * * * *

Joe Bridges of the Haywood County Sheriff's Office in Waynesville, North Carolina, called to report that the Waynesville Hospital might have treated Trenny Gibson on the night she disappeared.

A young girl who gave her name as Rita K. Gibson had been treated for cuts and bruises. After a thorough check, it was established that the girl who had been treated was a local girl.

The Intensive Search Ends

The Park Service had conducted an intensive search for Trenny from October 8, through October 22, 1976.

For the 756 searchers who toiled so hard, there was no happy ending, not even an ending. How she had vanished was as mysterious at the end of the search as it had been when it began.

Searchers had utilized sweep-line and grid methods to search a radius of three miles in all directions from the point where Trenny was last seen on the Andrews Bald Trail.

Walkers searched all major and minor trails, drainages and ridges between Andrews Bald and Elkmont in Tennessee, a distance of 15 miles, and Fontana Lake in North Carolina, a distance of 14 miles.

Although weary and worn, most of the searchers resolved to search again as much as their time permitted.

A Limited Search

After the intensive search ended on October 22, 1976, a limited search was conducted until November 2, 1976, when the Park Service ended the organized search. Ranger Linahan made a statement to the press:

"We have made a concentrated effort and done everything reasonable and prudent, but we can find no shred of physical evidence to show that Trenny Gibson is in the Park.

"The organized search is over, but we shall utilize our personnel in a maintenance search. This means they will be alert for evidence as a part of their regular overall duties and responsibilities."

Robert Gibson protested ending the search and told the press, "I shall work to reopen this search. No one in the Park Service has told us she is not in the Park.

"The FBI is still on the case, and they tell us they will leave no stone unturned.

"All we can do now is trust in God and the FBI. Faith has kept us going this far.

"I want to emphasize that our family appreciates the effort of the Park Service, the volunteers and everyone who did anything to help in the search for Trenny, and the kindness of everyone in Gatlinburg."

A Reward is Offered

Robert Gibson contacted his legislators to help him persuade Governor Ray Blanton of Tennessee to offer a reward for information about Trenny.

On November 5, 1976, Governor Blanton announced he was offering a $5,000 reward for information leading to the arrest and conviction of the person or persons responsible for the disappearance of Trenny Lynn Gibson.

It produced no leads. Robert Gibson contacted authorities about adding some family funds to increase the reward. The authorities said it would be futile.

The reward remained at $5,000. It is now 1998, and there has never been an inquiry about it.

The Aftermath

The 1976 holiday season was an especially sad time for Trenny's family. "We waited, in prayer and hope, the first few months," Hope Gibson explained. "The feeling of the unknown has had a great impact on us. Your life can't remain the same when a key member of your family is taken away. Our family has retreated into isolation but not entirely by choice. People don't know how to react to us in all this, so they're evidently trying to stay as far away as they can. Friends who used to come by just don't anymore. People who used to call have quit."

The family had attended Calvary Baptist Tabernacle in Knoxville at the time Trenny disappeared. Even this source of contact and comfort had lessened as time went by.

* * * * *

At the time Trenny disappeared, Robert Gibson was director of personnel development for Malter International Corporation and was required to travel about two weeks out of every month. He had asked for a job transfer, and his request had been granted.

Lobbying for a Second Search

Robert Gibson began applying unrelenting pressure on the Park Service to reopen the search. He contacted state and national government officials. Having worked for President Jimmy Carter, he prevailed upon him to intercede.

Hope Gibson did not join Robert in the push for a second search.

Ranger Jack Linahan was not convinced there was any reason to reopen the search. "If she was there, we would have found her."

The political pressure on the Park Service through the President paid off. The Gibsons were advised by the Park Service that they would conduct another search as soon as the mountains were clear of snow.

The Second Search for Trenny
April 18 - May 5, 1977

The second search for Trenny Gibson began shortly after 7:00 AM on April 18, 1977, with 13 searchers. Most were Park personnel assigned to search duty.

The weather was cold; and the mountains were shrouded in a heavy fog, with heavy rain and the possibility of snow flurries in the forecast. There were many icy spots at the higher elevations.

Robert Gibson was displeased at the small number of searchers. Ranger Linahan explained that most of the volunteers who had searched so long last October with totally negative results did not think a second search was worthwhile. They did not believe anything had been over looked. The rain moved in and the fog made it impossible to continue the search. It was terminated at 3:45 PM. Nothing had been found.

Bitter cold, rain and strong winds hampered the search for the next several days. The weather was so harsh on April 21 and April 23, no search could be undertaken. Because of the weather conditions, the original ending date of April 30 was extended through May 5, 1977.

Between April 18 and May 5, 1977, over 230 searchers braved the elements to participate in the search. No one found a trace of Trenny Gibson. It was, all over again, as if she had vanished into thin air.

The emotions expressed by the searchers ranged from frustration to resignation, but all shared a deep sense of disappointment. No one could think of any thing else to do. Every experienced searcher knows the Smoky Mountains are wild and full of places to conceal a body for years. They are too huge to search every inch, and the reality was the search had to end.

Several searchers were treated for exhaustion; and some were near victims of hypothermia, a condition caused by overexposure to cold weather. Dr. Robert Lash and his University of Tennessee Medical team administered treatment at the search site.

The Second Search Ends

On May 6, 1977, the National Park Service issued a news release on the second search for Trenny Gibson.

"The intensive search, renewed on April 18, 1977, in

the Clingmans Dome area of the Great Smoky Mountains National Park, where Trenny Gibson disappeared six months ago, has been completed.

"Searchers have again gone to great lengths in extremely rugged mountain areas to find any clues to Trenny's disappearance, but after extensive search no evidence has been found.

"The search will never end as long as Trenny is missing. Although the formal search phase is over, our personnel will continue to be alert for clues, or any evidence."

After the Second Search

Hope and Robert Gibson wrote letters to the local newspapers expressing their appreciation to everyone involved in the two searches for Trenny and to the many people who had been kind to them in their time of need and deep sorrow.

Robert Jr. was especially close to Trenny. He was on leave from the Navy at the time she disappeared. The Navy extended his leave for several weeks. After his extended leave expired, he returned to duty aboard the USS Ramsey; but he could not concentrate on his duties. The Navy granted him an honorable discharge.

Park officials had asked the family not to participate in the organized searches since they were not trained searchers and could get in difficulty in the mountains.

Two of Trenny's uncles had been persistent and had participated in the first search. Later on, these uncles and

other relatives of Mrs. Gibson, who came from mountain-
ous Polk County, Tennessee, brought their own search dogs
and searched for Trenny. Robert Jr. helped search until his
feet bled.

Sadly, the results of their searches were the same as
those of all the other searches. They found no trace of
Trenny.

* * * * *

There were many tough days after Trenny disappeared,
but one of the toughest was August 17, 1977, Trenny's 17th
birthday. The family did not dine out as was their usual
custom for birthdays. The vacation to Florida, planned for
July, was cancelled. They went to the Smoky Mountains
where Trenny might be.

The Gibsons File Suit

On September 26, 1977, Robert and Hope Gibson
filed suit against the City of Knoxville; City of Knoxville
Board of Education; James Newman, superintendent of
Knoxville City Schools; Frank Hall, principal of Bearden
High School; and Wayne Dunlap, the supervisor of the field
trip to the Clingmans Dome area.

The suit alleged negligence by the defendants which
resulted in their daughter Trenny Gibson being lost. They
asked for a jury trial and a judgment of $350,000 as
compensation for their loss.

The Gibsons listed specific emotional, medical and
financial damages to the individual family members. They
stated that the family bond had completely broken down

after Trenny disappeared. The suit never came to trial. On September 8, 1980, it was dismissed by the Circuit Court for Knox County for failure of the Gibsons to prosecute the matter.

Following Every Lead

The Gibsons received letters from several inmates in state prisons who claimed to have information about Trenny. They secured permission to interview these prisoners. Hope Gibson explained, "We would always pose as relatives so other prisoners would not know the prisoner we were visiting was 'snitching." All of the information from prisoners turned out to be hoaxes.

Robert Gibson checked with religious organizations in New York which have reputations for hiding young people. Nothing. He also discussed his daughter's disappearance with crime experts all over the county. The consensus among them was that she was abducted, probably by two or three men, taken out of the park, sexually assaulted and killed.

The Gibsons checked with bear experts and were informed that an extremely hungry bear can eat a person, clothes and all. If this does occur, some traces of the clothing may be found, even years later at a distant point, in the bear's feces.

These gruesome realities were overwhelming for the family. At funerals they would tell the surviving members of the deceased that while it is hard to bury a loved one, it is harder to carry the burden of the unknown forever.

The Gibsons in 1998

During the 22 years since Trenny disappeared, the Gibson family has ceased to exist as the unit it was in October 1976.

They sold the home in which they were living when Trenny disappeared, and the family moved together into another home.

Robert Gibson terminated his employment with Malter International and established Miracle Products Company in Knoxville.

Hope and Robert Gibson divorced in the mid-80s. Each married again. Robert's second marriages ended in divorce. Hope's husband died in 1993.

Robert Gibson married a third time. He lives in Ohio.

Hope is single. She left Knoxville, Tennessee, and established a home with Miracle, the youngest Gibson child. They both have full time jobs.

Tina lives in Tennessee. Robert Jr. lives in North Carolina.

Trenny?

Trenny walked away, alone, into the mist. Somehow she went beyond the reach of those who long to know, "Where did she go?"

Appendix A to Chapter 2
Trenny Lynn Gibson
See Appendix B for 2001 Update

After searching for over a year, Juanitta Baldwin located Trenny's mother, Hope Collins.

Mrs. Collins provided the photograph of Trenny which appears at the beginning of Chapter 2. She also wrote how she survived losing Trenny and how she has come to terms with this grim reality. What she wrote is published here, as she wrote it, with her permission.

* * * * *

August 17, 1998

Thirty eight years ago today precious Trenny came into this world. How I thank God for the sixteen glorious years he blessed my life with her presence.

My heart's desire and only purpose of having any part whatsoever in this book is to uplift, glorify, and magnify the name of my Lord and Saviour Jesus Christ. That through what few words I may write, God will use them to bless, encourage, and comfort the heart of some precious troubled, heartbroken soul.

God started preparing my heart in 1969 for what lay ahead. He gave me such hunger in my heart for his word. My husband won a Bible through the company he worked for at that time, an old 1611 King James Scofield Bible, the one I still carry, and study. My constant companion.

I would get up early to pray and study, then get the kids up for prayer, devotion, breakfast, then off to school.

Sundays and Wednesday nights we went to church at Calvary Baptist Tabernacle where Bro. Jim Seaton was our pastor. Every service was glorious, and such a blessing.

The year before Trenny vanished, anyone I went to church with will recall what I am going to tell you. I was so troubled, and under such burden, staying on the altar or behind the piano praying, asking people to pray, telling them that something bad was going to happen in my family. I had no idea what, nor to whom, but I knew to the bottom of my soul there was something going to happen.

It takes only a split second for our lives to be changed forever. We take life and its blessings for granted until something shakes our world.

I don't think there is anything on earth that could have been more hurtful, tragic, or devastating. No way can I imagine going through such heartache without Christ. What pain and suffering this has caused our entire family.

Never for a moment after that third day of the search for Trenny have I thought she was lost in the mountains.

Too many unanswered questions, but praise God, the day is coming when I'll have the answer to every question. Not only will I learn why Trenny's comb that she never, ever parted with was found in the car of a Friend? Or why that friend? was never allowed to be questioned, or why instead of walking back to the parking lot with her, after eating half of her lunch - went tracking a bear.

Oh, so many unanswered questions. However, I find the more I stay on my knees in prayer, the more God answers. You see, there are so many promises in God's Word that if we will just ask Mt. 7:7,8 Jh. 14:13,14 Jh 15:7. These are just a few. I keep praying for God to get hold of every heart of every person involved. I pray he will take their peace, take their rest. I pray they will never have another night of rest until they fall at the feet of the Lord Jesus Christ begging his forgiveness and ask him into their heart, and to take over their life.

* * * * *

For over twelve years after Trenny vanished, there was only one set of footprints in the sand, and many times since there's been only one set. I didn't cry. I couldn't. Didn't show any emotion, couldn't do that either. My body was alive. I went through all the motions of being alive, but inside my very soul had been torn out, just emptiness, sadness, and hurt. No one could comfort, no one even knew how or what to say. It seemed my prayers got nowhere, everything just a blank wall.

I can honestly say that I never blamed God, or questioned him, always I would remember his words in Romans 8:28 - And we know that all things work to- gether for good to them that love God, to them who are called according to his purpose. Also I knew that I had laid all my children on the altar for God, gave them back to him, told him they were his, and asked his will be done.

After Trenny disappeared, I couldn't turn around then and say "Well God, I didn't mean it that way." See a lot of times we want God's will done if its something that suits us. It doesn't work that way. Yes, I want God's will for my life. I wanted it then, and I haven't changed my mind today.

God brought me through that twelve years of wilderness. You see we may go through the fire, but he is there with us. Day by day he began breathing life back into my dead soul, and opening my eyes to see what he was doing in my life.

The mountain tops are wonderful, but it's the valleys where we get our strength, and learn to lean on Jesus. The day I started praying, dear God there has to be something good in all this. Please show me that good. That's the day he began a new work in me.

There are things that I feel a special gift from God, that he did just for me, so many times through the years I have been able to look back and draw strength from them. For instance the Sunday that just Trenny and I were in church. I don't remember now why the rest of the kids weren't with us because I always took all four kids, Bob Jr., Trenny, Tina and Miracle to every service, but this Sunday it was just the two of us.

When Bro. Jim got up to preach he said, "I believe we

ought to just have a love service. If there is somebody here who has been a blessing to your life, just go tell them you love them." Both Trenny and I started getting up at the same time, and in unison turning to each other with outstretched arms. I can still see in my mind's eye that precious little face, with tears streaming down her cheeks, saying "I love you, Mom" as we embraced. Oh Blessed Jesus, how I miss her!

Glory to God, I will see her again! This I know without doubt. All these years I had prayed just to know something, anything, just to know. Well last September our church had an ole fashion tent meeting. Oh how glorious all week long.

On about the fifth night, Bro. Harry Nix brought the message and after the service was over, everybody was just standing around visiting when I walked over to shake hands with the preacher's wife, and his sister, Sue. Sue started asking how old Trenny was when she disappeared. I started telling her - or at least I think so. Anyway, the sweet Holy Spirit of God swept through my soul, speaks the words to my heart, "You'll see her again!" Well glory, talk about one rejoicing, praising the Lord good time, I had it! Now I don't know if I'll see her in this life or when I step on the shores of glory, just that I will see her again!

What a joy it is to awake each morning to a brand new day, a day that never has been before, and never will be again. And God has allowed me to be right in the middle of it. Praise the Lord I'm alive. I'm alive! How I would love the whole world to know the same peace I feel in my soul.

I could go on and on telling you what God has done for me, how he blesses my life, and still not get it all told, but I am thankful for the privilege and opportunity to tell just a small part of how God took my all-to-pieces life and put it together again. Truly, truly, I give him all the praise, honor and glory. How I pray he will use my little part to touch and comfort whom he will.

God has taught me so many things through all the heartaches. I wish there was time and space. However, there is just one thing I must share. Have you ever met one of those people that worried about everything?

That was me. If there was nothing to worry about, I would certainly come up with something. Well, guess what? I don't worry about anything anymore.

It's a sin for a Christian to worry. I'm not saying there are not burdens to carry, or that I'm not concerned, there is a big difference. When I'm burdened, I go to the burden bearer. Ps. 55:22 tells me to cast my burden on the Lord. Matthew 11:28, 29, 30 tell me "Come unto me, all ye that labour and are heavy laden, and I will give you rest. Take my yoke upon you, and learn of me; for I am meek and lowly in heart; and ye shall find rest for your souls. For my yoke is easy, and my burden is light."

What more could anyone want? I have it all in the Lord Jesus Christ.

Appendix B to Chapter 2
Trenny Lynn Gibson - 2001 Update

Trenny's mother, Hope Gibson Collins, married Larry Vaughan, in 1999 and moved to West Virginia. They conduct a ministry for prisoners.

In December 2000, Trenny's brother, Robert Gibson, Jr. died of natural causes. Tina, Trenny's sister, is married and lives in Texas. Miracle, Trenny's younger brother, lives in Tennessee. Robert Gibson, Sr. lives in Tennessee.

Hope said, "Tell your readers that my faith is stronger than ever. I am very happy and so proud of my two children who are still with me. I believe Robert, Jr. is in Heaven, and Trenny is too, unless by some miracle she is alive. Some-body knows what happened to her. I pray that God will lay such a burden on their heart that they must tell.

"I repeat what I wrote back in 1998 - I don't know if I'll see her in this life or when I step on the shores of glory but I have peace because I know that I will see her again!"

Appendix C to Chapter 2
Trenny Lynn Gibson - 2009 Update

Hope Gibson is well and happy. She asks anyone who knows what happened to Trenny to please break their silence.

Chapter 3
Dennis Lloyd Martin

Dennis Lloyd Martin disappeared on June 14, 1969, six days before his seventh birthday, at Spence Field in Great Smoky Mountains National Park. The most intensive and longest search ever conducted for a lost person, to that date, failed to turn up any trace of him.

* * * * *

Dennis Martin loved the mountains. After he disappeared, his mother, Violet Martin, wrote to newspapers throughout the Southeast.

"Dennis begs to go to the mountains on weekends. He is an experienced mountain hiker for a seven-year-old, and is usually out in front of the group, picking up the trail. Please publish this photograph of Dennis, and ask anyone who might see a child fitting his description, and perhaps seeming to be 'out of place,' to please contact us, or the police."

When Dennis disappeared he was wearing a red T-shirt, dark green hiking shorts, white socks and black oxfords. He was described as about four feet tall, 55 pounds, dark brown, wavy hair, dark brown eyes with long, thick eyelashes, and missing one front tooth.

Dennis lived in Knoxville, Tennessee, with his parents, William and Violet Martin, brothers Douglas and Michael, sister Sarah, and Lady, a German shepherd. On the Saturday he disappeared he was on a weekend camping trip with his father, nine-year-old brother Douglas, and grandfather Clyde E. Martin, a Knoxville school teacher.

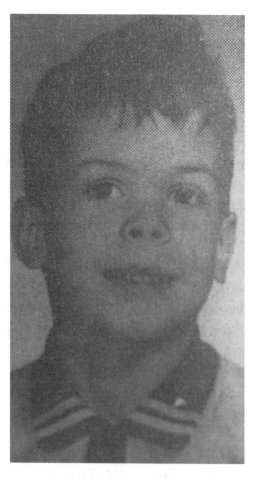

Dennis Lloyd Martin

The Martin Family Camping Trip

The camping trip began on Friday morning, June 13, 1969. William Martin, an architect, took the day off so he could have three days with his father and two sons to celebrate Father's Day. Camping in the Smokies was almost an annual event for them.

The Martins camped Friday night in Russell Field at the edge of the Appalachian Trail. Dennis and Douglas made friends with two boys from Alabama who were camping there with their parents. Ironically, their names were Carter Martin II, age 11, and Douglas Martin, 9. The two Martin families had never met before and are not related.

During Saturday, June 14, 1969, the two Martin families hiked together about two and a half miles east to Spence Field, a large, almost level clearing at 4800 foot elevation. The field is carpeted with thick grass and a few sparse clusters of scrub trees. Both Martin families planned to camp there on Saturday night. It had a hiking shelter, which was welcome because the day was hot and rain appeared likely.

About 4:00 PM, the four Martin boys were playing around the hiking shelter and near the Anthony Creek trail head. Dennis' father, William, and several other adults were seated in a grassy spot watching them. They saw the boys split up and run in different directions toward clumps of trees.

All the boys, except Dennis, slipped up in front of the adults making noises intended to scare them. When Dennis did not appear, his father became concerned and questioned the other three boys. Dennis' brother, Douglas, explained that the boys had planned to slip up on the adults and scare them. Dennis was to slip up from behind because he was wearing a bright red T-shirt which could be seen for a long way.

Within three to five minutes William Martin began calling his son's name. There was no response, and Dennis did not come out of the trees. He and the other adults began to search for him.

* * * * *

Dennis was close to the Anthony Creek trail head when he disappeared. The immediate concern was that he had become confused and might be headed down the wrong trail, away from Spence Field.

It was decided everyone would search Spence Field except Dennis' father. He hiked to Russell Field and back. Neither he nor the searchers in Spence Field found any trace of Dennis.

The state line between Tennessee and North Carolina runs along the apex of Spence field along the Appalachian Trail. Anthony Creek and Bote Mountain trails on the Tennessee side and Eagle Creek and Jenkins Ridge trails on the North Carolina side have trail heads at Spence Field. Bote Mountain Trail has 5.5 miles available for truck use, and the last 1.5 miles to Spence Field is for jeep travel only.

The seasonal Park naturalist, Terry Chilcoat and his wife arrived at Spence Field shortly after Dennis vanished.

They had driven the 5.5 miles of Bote Mountain Trail and hiked the remaining 1.5 miles to Spence Field but had not seen Dennis.

Dennis' Grandfather Goes For Help

Dennis' grandfather Clyde Martin hiked down Anthony Creek Trail to get help. He arrived at Cades Cove about 8:30 PM and told Park Ranger Larry K. Nielson what had happened. Ranger Nielson immediately called for help and started back to Spence Field with Clyde Martin.

Darkness fell as they made their way up the mountain. Heavy thunderstorms with fierce lightning made travel very difficult. The temperature began to drop.

Several park rangers made their way to Spence Field. They joined those searching the area where Dennis was last seen. All night they slogged through the grass and undergrowth, crawling at times on their hands and knees.

Over two inches of rain fell on Spence Field during the night, and the temperature dropped to about 50 degrees. All gullies and streams had become high and turbulent, and this hampered the search.

Experienced rangers consoled the family with the fact that Dennis would be cold, wet, and no doubt frightened, but he could survive in the present weather conditions.

Not one single clue as to where Dennis could have gone was found during that night.

Chief Ranger M. Sneddon worked during Saturday night to set up a contingency search plan. A search camp would be set up at Spence Field. A helicopter was secured to transport personnel and supplies there because the heavy rain had made the Bote Mountain Trail very difficult to negotiate.

Park rangers and maintenance personnel, rescue squads from Sevier and Blount counties, the Smoky Mountain Hiking Club, and many individuals experienced in searching in the Smokies were contacted and asked to be at the foot of Bote Mountain Trail in Cades Cove at 5:00 AM unless they were called not to come.

Dennis was not found, and the search plan was put into action on Sunday, June 15, 1969. By 10:00 AM, over 100 searchers were looking for Dennis.

* * * * *

Violet Martin was not notified that Dennis was missing until Sunday morning. The Martin family were members of Vestal United Methodist Church in Knoxville. Violet and their two younger children went to Sunday School as usual. Rev. George Armbrister, pastor of the church, was notified and broke the news to her. She arrived at the search site about noon.

Rev. Armbrister also announced the sad news to those attending Sunday School. Many of those attending church that morning left immediately to offer their help.

Spence Field Searched Again

Spence Field, and the surrounding area, was searched again after daylight came on Sunday morning. The searchers found nothing. Local newspapers and radio stations reported that a six year old boy was missing in the Great

Smoky Mountains National Park. Offers of help flooded into Park Headquarters. The roads into the search area had to be closed to keep out the curious.

Over 150 additional qualified searchers made their way through the traffic. After being screened for fitness by Park officials, they were assigned to the areas where Dennis was most likely to be found.

The Red Cross had been contacted and arrived with more than ample food and drink for the searchers. The ladies of Townsend, Tennessee, had brought food and drinks to the Cades Cove Ranger Station.

All of this was in addition to the emergency rations supplied by the Park Service. There was an overabundance of food supplied by volunteers throughout the long and grueling search for Dennis.

At sundown on Sunday, over 250 well-trained searchers were walking the trails and crisscrossing the areas in between. The search was suspended because of heavy rain and darkness. No clue about Dennis' disappearance had been found.

The Magnitude of the Search Increases

The magnitude of the search grew as the news was picked up by the national media. On Monday, there were 300 searchers, many with equipment such as jeeps, portable radios, maps, and tracking supplies. This challenged the capacity of the search coordinator to utilize everyone and everything safely and effectively.

A heliport was established at Cades Cove to transport

personnel, equipment, and supplies to Spence Field. Sporadic rain kept the Bote Mountain road muddy. The heavier than normal traffic was rutting it badly, making travel on it slow and dangerous.

Five dog handlers worked at intervals during Monday but could not pick up Dennis' trail.

When the search ended on Monday, plans had been made for fresh searchers to relieve those suffering from fatigue. Military units, civilian groups, and TVA personnel were expected on Tuesday, which would be the third day of the search.

An Emotional Day

On the third day after Dennis vanished, a grim reality began to set in. The parents and family were trying to cling to hope but were emotionally exhausted.

There seemed to be a general feeling among some of the searchers that Dennis may have been a victim of the wild boars which had invaded the section of the Park where he was last seen. The boars, a wild hog imported from Europe to the Tellico, Tennessee, area half a century ago had spread into the Park.

Ronald Lauter, a veteran woodsman, said evidence of heavy boar activity was found. If Dennis had encountered a vicious sow with her young, it could have been fatal with little or no evidence remaining. All animal excrement was checked but none yielded anything to connect it to a human.

Putting hope above all else, the search coordinators transported about 300 searchers by jeeps and trucks up the muddy Bote Mountain Trail. The fog was so thick the helicopters could not fly until after 11:00 AM. When they could fly, they transported 65 more searchers and supplies to Spence Field.

The 365 searchers toiled on Tuesday, June 17, 1969, first in the fog, then in the steamy conditions brought on by the sporadic rain.

An intensive grid search was made at Spence Field. The searchers used plastic ribbons to mark the grid search areas. One color was placed around the perimeter of the area to be searched, and when the search was completed another color was put in place. All drainages around Spence Field were rechecked.

* * * * *

Late on Tuesday afternoon, hope flared when a radio station broadcast a report that "Dennis has been found." A reporter had overheard a radio report by a Park ranger to Park Headquarters that 'the little boy had been found.'

The little boy in this report was not Dennis Martin but another boy who was fishing in the Park with his grandfather. The grandfather had left the boy beside the stream to go dig more fishing worms.

When he came back, his grandson was gone. The grandfather turned in a lost-boy alarm, and a Park ranger responded. By the time the ranger arrived at the fishing spot, the grandson had returned. The ranger radioed Headquarters that the 'little boy' had been found but did not speak his name. This was the report a reporter had heard and jumped to the conclusion that the 'little boy' was Dennis.

Another flurry of excitement occurred when a shoe print and a footprint were found. Park rangers checked the size with the Martins, who said they were too large.

These and other similar incidents kept the Martin family and searchers on an emotional roller coaster during much of the long, exhausting search.

The Fourth Day

The total search force for Wednesday, June 18, 1969, the fourth day after Dennis disappeared, was 615.

Jeanne Dixon, a well known psychic in Washington, DC, sent a message where Dennis could be found. This was the first of dozens of calls from psychics, clairvoyants, and persons who believe they have the ability to 'see' or 'predict' things beyond the normal sensory perceptional range of average persons.

Jeanne Dixon said searchers should look around the area where Dennis was last seen playing. "He went out on level ground, went down an incline and turned off to the left at a 40-50 degree angle and up a little. He was walking, did not stumble or fall. Then he went back down and would be underneath the point of incline. The area where he turned left has shrubbery and is thickety. I do not see any trees where he veered off to left, more or less bare ground," she said. The Martins were very receptive to Ms. Dixon's call and all other similar calls. They played a definite part in how the search for Dennis was conducted.

The area specified by Jeanne Dixon had been searched many times, but it was searched again. Dennis was not where Jeanne Dixon had 'seen' him.

The Fifth Day

By the fifth day, many searchers were too tired to continue and did not report to search on June 19, 1969. But amazingly, newcomers arrived until the search force swelled to 690. Many of them came with a feeling of urgency. If Dennis Martin had managed to survive, he must be found quickly.

Trail shelters, pit toilets and fire towers were checked. Buzzards lead one group of searchers to a small dead animal. All search reports for June 19, 1969, were negative.

A Tennessee Highway Patrol helicopter flew William Martin over the search area, and he called to his son with a bullhorn. He could not be heard above the engine noise. Other helicopters were considered but the noise level on all of those available was too great.

From the first day, searchers had called Dennis' name because Mr. Martin said he was a quiet boy who probably would not call out but would answer if he heard his name. Dennis was in a special education group at school, as his mental age was about half a year behind his chronological age.

Public Relations

Media coverage continued to be extensive. Local newspapers and television stations kept reporters and photographers at the Park. One Park Service employee was assigned to handle press and public relations.

By Friday, June 20, 1969, the number of 'sightseers' had become a serious problem throughout the Park. Most of the roads in the Park had to be closed to the public so they could be used for transporting bona fide searchers and equipment. Between 35 and 40 persons were required for traffic control around the clock.

Many individuals, with good intentions but no training in search and rescue work, came to volunteer their services. For safety reasons, they could not be utilized; and this became a public relations nightmare for Park officials.

Media reports went out about volunteers being turned away. Angry telephone calls flooded the Park Headquarters, and a few persons came to the Park to protest in person. Others contacted the media with their complaints. In an attempt to stop the erroneous information, Chief Ranger Sneddon issued an urgent press release.

He requested that no individuals or groups come to the search area without prior consultation. He expressed his sincere appreciation for all the help and explained that the number of searchers committed to come to the area had reached the saturation point.

So far injuries during this search had been remarkably light. Chief Sneddon pled for persons to cooperate to keep it that way. The most serious injury to date had been a broken arm sustained when a searcher fell while trying to cross an abandoned bridge.

The search operation had become publicly significant, and nationwide interest developed quickly. Politicians from

Tennessee contacted the Park Service Headquarters and officials at the search site.

Officials from the White House contacted the National Park Service to ascertain that all logical possibilities were satisfactorily accounted for in the minds of the parents and all those concerned.

* * * * *

Searchers were briefed on two plans, A and B, as to what to do when Dennis Martin was found.

Plan A gave them specific instructions what to do if Dennis was found alive. Plan B was what to do if he was found dead. Neither Plan A or Plan B was ever needed.

Consoling and Informing Dennis' Parents

The Martins were kept fully informed of everything that was being done to find their son. They spent a lot of time at the search site and conferred with search officials, the media and searchers as they chose.

Time and the weather had not been favorable for Dennis' survival. Park officials and experienced searchers were candid with the parents that the chances of Dennis being found alive decreased with each hour.

There was little that could be said to console the distraught parents, but they seemed to take comfort in the almost superhuman efforts being made to find their son, dead or alive.

* * * * *

Almost a week had passed since Dennis had vanished. Hope for him being found alive was growing dim. The total absence of any clue fueled speculation that Dennis had been kidnapped.

The Martins were plagued by the possibility that someone could have gotten the two Martin families present at Spence Field that afternoon mixed up and kidnapped the wrong boy.

Suspicions that some of the searchers may have found Dennis and whisked him away were expressed. These speculations and suspicions, according to Park Service officials experienced in dealing with the families of missing persons, are inevitable. They reflect fear and deep-seated resistance to accepting the possibility that what actually happened may never be known.

The Martins asked the Park Service to call in the Federal Bureau of Investigation, and this was done. The FBI advised that no evidence had been found to support kidnapping.

Until some evidence was developed, the FBI could not launch a full-scale investigation but would check any lead that might develop. No leads which pointed to a possible kidnapping ever developed.

The Sixth Day

The sixth day of the search, Friday, June 20, 1969, was beset with thunderstorms. More jeeps and helicopters arrived but could not be fully utilized. Records show 780 searchers braved the elements as best they could on foot. The search was suspended at dusk.

In six days, 12.5 square miles had been searched

intensively, and over 56 miles had been searched generally. This more than covered the logical search area where Dennis could have gone under his own power.

End of the First Week

As the end of the first week after Dennis Martin had vanished approached, hope of finding him was almost gone. On Saturday, June 21, 1969, 1400 searchers toiled in the steam which rose unmercifully between the heavy thunderstorms. Their toil was in vain.

Nothing had been found, but the search would be continued.

The Second Week

On Sunday, June 22, 1969, the search force totaled just over 1000. The weather was clear and helicopters flew almost all day. On the ground, the search began at Spence Field, and the area was thoroughly searched again.

The number of 'sightseers' decreased significantly. Radio and TV stations were informed that the road blocks to Cades Cove Campground and other Park facilities would be removed after all search crews had departed on Sunday night. All search reports were negative.

Second Monday

The weather closed in on Monday, June 23, 1969. Heavy rains curtailed all search efforts for most of the day. Helicopters could not fly.

The search force of 427 was sheltered in tents at Spence Field. They spent a frustrating day listening to the dismal weather reports and rushing out each time the rain stopped only to be driven back to their tents.

A police dog and his handler from the Spartanburg, South Carolina, Police Department attempted a search but could not pick up a scent.

Second Tuesday

By Tuesday morning, June 24, 1969, the weather had improved. A force of 482 searchers worked from dawn to dusk with negative results.

Two dog owners arrived and volunteered to attempt tracking Dennis. They were given permission, but neither dog could track him.

During the afternoon, a young boy wearing a red T-shirt and green short pants was seen walking the perimeter road at the Cades Cove Campground. Rangers investigated. The boy was Michael Devlin, who was camping with his parents in the Cades Cove Campground. The situation was explained to the parents who immediately agreed to have Michael change his shirt.

Second Wednesday

The search force on Wednesday, June 25, 1969, was 403. They found nothing.

After the search ended that day, the Park Service issued a press release. The search for Dennis would be greatly reduced beginning the next day.

The reduced search would be conducted from June 26 through June 29, 1969. If Dennis Martin was not found by June 29, 1969, the reduced search would be terminated. After June 29, 1969, a limited search would be conducted for up to 60 days.

Second Thursday

On Thursday, June 26, 1969, 121 searchers tried to find Dennis but could not.

Harold Key, 45, from Carthage, Tennessee, called Park Headquarters. He said he had been in the Park on the Saturday afternoon Dennis disappeared but was not sure of his exact location. He was walking in the woods when he heard a loud scream and glimpsed a man hiding in the bushes. A white car, with no one in it, had been parked close to where he had parked. When he returned to his car, the white car was gone.

Park officials ascertained that Mr. Key was in the Sea Branch area, which is over five miles from where Dennis disappeared. That area had been searched intensively before Mr. Key made his report.

Second Friday

On Friday, June 27, 1969, the thirteenth day into the full search, a force of 68 looked for Dennis from dawn to dusk with negative results.

A man identifying himself as Billy Noland, a psychic interpreter from New Orleans, Louisiana, came to Park Headquarters and spoke with the Martins. He told them he was positive he could find Dennis and headed for Rocky Top on the Appalachian Trail.

He returned, without finding a single clue about Dennis, but told the Martins he was still quite positive that all he needed was a little time. He actually needed funds, food and shelter. No one chose to finance Mr. Noland's search.

Second Saturday

Saturday, June 28, 1969, brought out volunteers who had heard the search would be terminated the next day. The search force was 196.

The Last Day of the Intensive Search

Sunday, June 29, 1969, was a day of hope and pathos for the Martins, Park officials, all searchers, but especially the 318 at the scene who had given it their last, best shot.

By 6:00 PM on June 29, 1969, all searchers and equipment had been brought down from the mountains. The intensive search was over.

The Limited Search

On June 30, 1969, Rangers Arthur Whitehead, Grady Whitehead, and J. R. Buchanan, all of whom were intimately familiar with the area where Dennis vanished, were assigned full-time duty to continue the search.

They searched for two and one-half months, but did not find anything.

The Martins Offer a Reward

Dennis Martin's parents offered a $5,000 reward for information leading to his safe return. They prepared a flyer with pertinent information and three photos of Dennis on it. It was widely distributed.

The reward produced no viable leads and has never been claimed.

Forty Years Have Past

It has been almost 40 years since Dennis Martin ran into a clump of bushes and vanished.

The search for him began within five minutes. It was daylight. He was with his family who loved him. They heard no sounds, saw no strangers or animals.

His family is left to ponder "How can this be?"

Experienced searchers accept a sad and sobering truth. The Smokies are full of secrets they refuse to yield to mere mortals.

The unsolved disappearance of Dennis Martin is one of them.

Part II
Puzzlers

Edward (Edd) McKinley
Abe Carroll Ramsey

* * * * *

An unidentified boy was found frozen to
death in 1915, and buried by kind strangers.
His identity was a mystery for 60 years.

* * * * *

Abe Ramsey, age 3, wandered away from his
home on March 11, 1919. The story that he
was never found may not be true.

Chapter 4
Edward (Edd) McKinley
Preface

There is a sad story about an unknown redheaded boy found frozen to death in the Great Smoky Mountains in 1915. The kind strangers who found him took him to the Sugarlands Community. They tried for three days to identify him but could not. The residents then banded together and buried him.

The story is that it took 60 years to solve the mystery of the boy's identity. We selected this story for this book because it was a mystery which had been solved.

Almost immediately in our research, we chanced upon information which raised the question: How could Edward McKinley's identity have remained a mystery for 60 years? And why?

After delving into these questions for months, we found an intriguing explanation. Consequently, we have written the Edward McKinley mystery in two sections.

Section A tells the Edward McKinley story as it has been told and written since 1915.

Section B is the intriguing explanation we found as to how, and why, Edward McKinley's identity was a mystery to so many people for over 60 years.

Section C reports details we have learned, thanks to our readers, about Edward's fateful journey since this book published in 1998 and this update in 2001.

Edward McKinley with his Family - 1913
Edward is in the front row, right end

Front row: George McKinley, Mary Whitehead McKinley holding Virgie, Bruce, Bonnie, Roy, and Edward.

Back row: Albert Boone, Martha McKinley Boone holding Virgil, Minnie McKinley Huffstetler holding Nellie, Will, and Albert.

Photograph courtesy Betty Boone Best. Edward is her great uncle.

Chapter 4
Edward (Edd) McKinley
Section A

Joe and Jim Cole were cousins. In 1915, they lived in the Sugarlands area on the Tennessee side of the Great Smoky Mountains. There had been snow over Easter weekend, but by Wednesday it had melted off except in the dense shade. It was cold, but the bright sunlight made it a good day to go hunting.

A few greens were poking up in the meadow. Maybe there was enough for a good mess. Fresh greens would taste better with fresh meat, they told each other as they left home. They laughed. Any excuse was a good excuse to go hunting.

They left early, hiking toward Deep Creek on the North Carolina side of the Smokies. They met a couple of other hunters and a man on his way to fish, but they did not join up with them. Their plan was to shoot what they could on the way back from Deep Creek, so as not to have so far to carry their find.

Before the first shot was fired, they came upon the dead body of a handsome young boy. He was beside a leaning rock where he had tried to seek shelter. Cold rocks and wet sticks close to his hands told the Cole cousins he had tried but failed to build himself a fire.

Although they knew everyone for miles around, this boy, with thick red hair and freckles, was a stranger. They could not fathom why he was here all alone. Perhaps someone back in the Sugarlands settlement would know him. They decided not to go inquiring at the few cabins further down on Deep Creek. They would send back word if need be.

Having dealt with injuries suffered by persons working and hunting in the uninhabited mountains, the Coles knew what to do. They constructed a lizard to carry the body. A lizard is a rough, but adequate, version of a sled. To make it, they cut a young tree with strong forked limbs. The body was placed in the fork and tied securely to each side using ties made from part of the clothing the boy was wearing.

Good Samaritans

The Cole cousins dragged the body to the Old Indian Road, the only road that crossed the crest of the Smoky Mountains, and began their arduous journey home. The road had been built during the Civil War and had never been maintained. It was narrow and rocky in the best spots, deeply rutted and muddy.

Shortly after they crossed back into Tennessee, they stopped to speak with Goldie Brown who lived in a cabin at Indian Grave Flats. He recognized the dead boy and told them what he knew about him.

This young boy had come to his cabin about four days ago, just before dark. It was snowing very hard. He was cold, wet and hungry. The boy told Goldie he had stopped at another house but they had refused to let him in. Goldie did not know his name, where he was from, or exactly where he was headed. Goldie had given him food and made a pallet in front of the fireplace so he could lie down to rest and dry his clothing.

About an hour later, the boy was ready to go on. Goldie said he urged him to rest and sleep by the fire until the next day because crossing the mountains in a snowstorm was very dangerous. But the boy had said he thought he could make it okay, that he wanted to cross over the mountains.

Goldie said he could not persuade the boy to stay but told him if he saw it was too rough to turn around and come back. He did not come back.

The Cole cousins arrived at the Sugarlands community about midnight, exhausted from dragging the body across the mountains. It was very cold. They found a spot with enough snow to cover the body and to shelter it from the sun.

A Caring Community

The next morning word of the dead boy spread rapidly throughout the Sugarlands Community. Most of the residents came to view the body. No one knew the boy or had any idea who he might be or where he might have lived.

Passersby were asked to tell everyone they met about the dead boy. People came from miles around to look at the body, but no one could identify him.

An early spring was breaking in the Smokies, bringing sun and rain. The boy's body could not be kept because the snow pack around it was melting. On the third day, the residents banded together to bury this unfortunate boy known only to God.

Eli Huskey and Mack McCarter made a coffin of pine wood. The boy's clothing had been cut to make strips to tie him to the lizard. David Ogle did not think it fitting to bury him in cut clothes, so he supplied a new pair of bib overalls and a shirt from his store.

Men and boys of the community dug a grave for him beside the gate in the Sugarlands Cemetery. The unknown boy was laid to rest with a proper funeral by kind strangers. A big grey back rock was placed at the head and another at the foot of his grave. The final act of goodness that day was decorating the grave with yellow daffodils and handmade crepe paper flowers.

Sugarlands Community Passes into History

The Sugarlands community passed into history when the Great Smoky Mountains National Park was created in 1930. The residents gradually moved away; but the Sugarlands Cemetery, which had also become known as the Ogle Cemetery, and all other cemeteries, were preserved.

The sad tale of the unknown boy in the grave between the two grey back rocks was passed down from generation to generation of families uprooted and scattered away from the Sugarlands.

60 Years Later

Around Memorial Day in 1975, a woman came to the Suglarlands Visitor Center in the Great Smoky Mountains National Park and spoke with Glenn Cardwell, a long time

Park employee. She told him she was looking for the grave of her brother who had frozen to death in the Smokies over 60 years ago and had been buried somewhere in the Sugarlands.

The woman identified herself as Virgie Fowler Smith from Knoxville, Tennessee, and told a heart wrenching story. She said she was about five years old when her brother disappeared. Her mother had grieved for her lost son and had often talked with her about it.

Virgie said she was there to fulfill a lifelong intention to find where her brother was buried, long delayed by the pressures of life.

Glenn Cardwell had never heard this story. Another employee recalled that a letter had been received several years before giving an account of an unknown boy who had been found frozen to death and buried in the Sugarlands graveyard. The letter was located in the Park files.

This is a reproduction of the letter written by Mrs. Lucinda Ogle to the National Park Service.

Monday, Feb. 9th (1970)

Dear Folks,

With the news of the lost boy today - I remembered one time some one wanting to know at the Park of any lost folks before. And too, someone may have already told this happening. But Earnest, my husband was telling me about the young man they found when he was about 10 years old. He is almost 64 yrs. old now so that would be 53 or 4 years ago.

The boy was about 21 years old * (see footnote) - red headed and freckled faced. Had started across Old Smoky and stopped on the Newfound Gap Trail at the Goldy Brown Cabin (Champion Fiber homesteader cabin). It being near dark and beginning to snow, the keeper asked him to lay in front of the fire until morning. But the boy said he thought he could make it across before it got too bad.

A few days later a hunting group which included Joe Cole (father of Kyle Cole) found the boy frozen to death, down on Deep Creek, N. C.. He had missed the main trail and followed a hunting trail.

They carried him back to this side of the mountain, to bury him in the Sugarlands graveyard. Earnest's father, Dave Ogle, give a new pair of overalls out of his store. Eli Huskey and some others made a wooden coffin.

Earnest said he helped dig the grave. This is one unmarked grave with grey back stones, located near the entrance to the graveyard. No one ever knew who he was.

I have scribbled this as Earnest told me, so I hope you can make out as he told it.

Sincerely,

Lucinda Ogle

* There are discrepancies about Edward's age in the oral and written accounts. Virgie Smith ultimately settled on his birthday as March 10, 1903.

* * * * *

Lucinda Ogle's letter was the link needed to connect Virgie Smith with persons who could help her.

Glenn Cardwell called the Ogles and arranged for Virgie to visit them in their home in Gatlinburg, Tennessee.

It was a happy occasion all around. After comparing notes, they were each convinced that the redheaded boy was Virgie Smith's brother, whose name was Edward McKinley. She cried with joy at the realization that she could fulfill her long-standing intention to visit his grave.

For the Ogles, the mystery of the unknown boy who had frozen to death in the Smokies over 60 years ago was solved during this visit. Virgie made many subsequent visits to the Ogle home and told them details of life in Edward McKinley's family.

Edward McKinley's Family

Their parents, George and Mary McKinley, had moved from Robinsville, North Carolina, to Blount County, Tennessee, before Edward was born. They lived in a rural area between Montvale Springs and Townsend.

George worked as a logger, probably for the Little River Lumber Company. The family planted a garden, kept a cow and raised hogs to help feed the family. The children were assigned chores to help keep the large household functioning.

Edward ran away when he was 13. There were nine children in the family at the time. Two daughters were married and had babies of their own.

Virgie said her father had a hot, quick temper and was very strict with all his children, especially the boys. He ruled the family and meted out verbal and corporal punishment at the slightest provocation. Her mother never questioned or opposed his decisions and actions. Even the slightest word from her mother was interpreted as questioning his authority, and he unleashed his wrath. This made matters worse. Mary McKinley found submission more tolerable than confrontation.

All the children were strong-willed, and conflicts were common in daily life. With Edward, it was a case of like father, like son. He had thick red hair and a temper to match. The girls, by and large, followed their mother's example of submission.

During March 1915, George had punished Edward severely for doing things that did not suit him. Edward resented what he believed to be unfair treatment and flared up at George more than once. On each occasion, George had thrashed Edward into submission.

The final confrontation between father and son was on March 28, 1915, the best the family can recall.

The Fateful Day

The McKinley home was heated with a small, two-eyed, wood-burning stove. The wood had to be cut into short and narrow sticks.

On a morning in March 1915, believed to be the 28th, Edward was trying to force a stick of wood into the eye of the stove. No matter which way he turned it, it was too big. His temper flared. He kicked the stick as hard as he could.

It did not go in, but the stove turned over almost setting the house on fire.

George McKinley thrashed Edward so harshly he rebelled. "I ain't sucking on the hind tit no more!" Edward shouted defiantly, jumping away to face his father.

This outburst shocked his father into speechlessness. An ominous silence hung between them for a few seconds. Despite his temper, Edward had accepted parental domination without open rebellion; but beneath his yielding exterior lurked a mulish core.

"As long as you eat at my table and sleep under my roof, you'll do what I say. No boy of mine is going to buck me," his father shouted. His slightly protruding eyes were naked as flint. "Now, get to splittin' wood. Make sure what you cut will go in the stove!"

Edward, aghast at his own daring, fell silent. Instead of more thrashing as he expected, his father walked past him and out of the house. A moment later, he stuck his head in the door to deliver a threatening volley, "I aim to give you the lickin' of your life when I get home!"

Edward looked squarely into his father's eyes but said nothing. Mary McKinley had witnessed George thrashing Edward and heard the angry exchange. She sensed this conflict was serious.

After George was out of earshot, she pleaded, "Son, please don't sass your Pa. It just makes trouble for all of us."

Usually, Edward was persuaded by her pleas, but today it only added to his misery. "It ain't fair. Why can't I ...?"

The distress on his mother's face silenced him. He shook his head and stomped toward the woodpile. About midway, he broke his stride to look back at his mother standing on the kitchen steps. She lifted her hand and smiled. He lifted his hand slightly and stomped on to the woodpile.

It was barely daylight. There was fog swirling about. Spring was breaking early and turbulently this year, so it was not too cold. He sat down on the chopping block to sharpen the axe. His brothers always left the axe dull. Here he was, sucking on the hind tit again. Anger turned to rage, festering with each stroke of the whetstone across the edge of the axe.

Rage overturned habit. "I'll find me another roof," he vowed to the sun topping over the Smoky Mountains. As soon as he was sure his father was gone for good, he stood and looked around. Slowly he laid the axe and the whet-stone on the chopping block, then went back into the house.

Several of his brothers and sisters were in the house, still shaken from the near catastrophe and confrontation. Edward told them he was going to his paternal grandmother's home. This grandmother's name was Elizabeth Prince McKinley. She lived in Cherokee, North Carolina, about forty miles away. (Note: Many records show that his grandmother lived in Cherokee County, but that is incorrect; she lived in Cherokee, North Carolina.)

Edward's siblings did not take him seriously and did not tell their mother.

On that foggy morning in March 1915, Edward McKinley walked away from his home. He would never return.

After Edward Ran Away

Virgie said she remembered her father and brothers searching for Edward for about two days. One of the brothers finally told their father that Edward had said he was going to his grandmother's home. They stopped searching, and the family felt relieved. In those days, communication was by word of mouth and mail.

The mail was very slow, so no one expected to hear from the grandmother with news about Edward for several weeks. Life, Virgie said, continued in almost a routine fashion. Except, she recalled with tears, for her mother's fear that something terrible had happened to Edward. She shared her fear with everyone in the family except George.

* * * * *

Virgie's recollection about the time frame when the family heard about Edward was hazy because of her tender age, just about five. Some family members told her that word came in about a month about a redheaded boy who had been found frozen to death on Deep Creek in North Carolina. Other family members think it was months before they heard about the boy.

By the time word came from Edward's grandmother that he had not reached her home, Virgie's parents had already learned that Edward had been found frozen to death and buried in the Sugarlands, but she did not know they learned this.

Earnest and Lucinda were astounded at what Virgie told them.

George McKinley's Edict

The parents did not share the details of what they had learned but simply told the children that Edward would not be coming back because he was dead. George McKinley issued an edict forbidding anyone in the family to ever talk about Edward.

They were forbidden to mention his name, even to each other. No one was to tell anyone, inside or outside of the family, what had happened to him. The fear of George McKinley enforced his edict of silence.

Virgie could not explain this most unusual behavior except to say that her father had a big family to feed, things were tough. It had been one of the worst winters in a long time, making logging work scarce. Since Edward was already buried, there was nothing he could do. He was afraid the people who had buried him might want to be paid.

Three more children were born to George and Mary

McKinley after Edward died. They were Ray, Melvin and Rosa. Because of the edict of silence, these three children did not know anything about Edward for many years. They might never have known if George McKinley had not left home one day, never to return.

He was never heard from again, so no one knows why he left, where he went or where he died.

Mary Whitehead McKinley was left with several small children to raise. Somehow she accomplished the daunting challenge and lived until the 1940s. She is buried in Knox County, Tennessee.

Virgie told the Ogles that her mother's grief for Edward lasted until the day she died. She longed to talk with the people who had buried the redheaded boy just to be sure it was Edward. But she had no money, no way to travel and so many children to raise all alone that she could never find the strength or the resources for such an undertaking.

Fulfilling a Lifelong Intention

Although the years had slipped away, Virgie expressed her gratitude at finding the Ogles and wanted to hear every detail Earnest Ogle could remember.

Earnest Ogle told Virgie he believed he was the only person still alive who had helped dig the grave and was present at Edward's funeral. If only she had come earlier, so many persons would not have gone to their graves wondering whose child they had helped to bury.

He recounted how word had been sent far and wide in the hope of finding the dead boy's family. People had come on horseback, and some had walked for miles. When they could keep the body no longer, the boy had been laid to rest with respect as if he had been one of their own. The boy in the unmarked grave was always remembered on decoration day when people took flowers to the cemetery before the Sugarlands became part of the Great Smoky Mountains National Park. He recalled seeing crepe paper flowers and some roses on the grave.

Virgie thanked the Ogles for their kindness in telling her about her long-lost brother. She also asked them to convey her family's appreciation to the descendants of the families who had shown compassion for Edward.

Earnest and Lucinda went with Virgie to the Sugarlands Cemetery, which by 1975 had also become known as the Sugarlands-Ogle Cemetery. She stood beside the grave between the two grey back rocks and said good-bye to Edward, whom she called Edd.

* * * * *

Some months later, Virgie obtained permission from the National Park Service to install a proper marble headstone to mark Edward's grave in the Sugarlands Cemetery.

The Sugarlands Cemetery cannot be reached by car. The road which existed when Edward was buried has become a trail. Virgie and one of her sons drove as close to the Cemetery as possible. Her son carried the marker on his shoulders the rest of the way to Edward's grave. The Ogles came and helped install the marker.

The inscription on the marker told the world that the

unknown boy buried between the grey back rocks was Edward (Edd) McKinley.

Edd McKinley
Born March 10, 1903
Died April 2, 1915

If the birth date on the marker is accurate, Edward had turned 12 on March 10, 1915. Whatever his age, he had an indomitable spirit to undertake walking across the Great Smoky Mountains alone in a snowstorm at night

Ester Grubb trekked to Edward McKinley's grave in July 1998. It was ominously quiet. While photographing his grave, she recalls thinking, "If only he could tell me everything that happened."

Chapter 4
Edward (Edd) McKinley
Section B

The news that the 60 year mystery of the identity of the boy who froze to death in the Great Smoky Mountains in 1915 had been solved was published in *The Knoxville News-Sentinel* on July 13, 1975.

Carson Brewer, a columnist for that newspaper and well-known writer about the Smokies, told the story in his July 13, 1975, column *This is YOUR Community*. He reported the mystery had been solved when Virgie Smith, the dead boy's sister, had gone to the Sugarlands Visitor Center searching for his grave. She was put in touch with Earnest and Lucinda Ogle who knew where the unknown boy was buried.

In his column on August 3, 1975, Mr. Brewer expanded the story. A man named Walter Diehl had been on a camping trip in the Smokies in April 1915. In June, Davis Brackens, a local, told him the boy who froze to death was not more than one-half mile from our camp. We had seen signs of footprints on our way to Indian Gap."

All the written accounts we found until 1998 told that no one had known the identity of the red-haired boy for over 60 years. We continued researching it and made an astounding discovery!

An Astounding Discovery

Juanitta Baldwin discovered a notice which had been published in a newspaper on April 14, 1915, in Sevierville, Tennessee.

Below is a constructed reproduction of the notice. We added the black box for emphasis.

The newspaper is on Microfilm Reel Number SE-M-91 at the Sevier County Library, Sevierville, Tennessee.

MONTGOMERY'S VINDICATOR
Sevierville, Tennessee, Wednesday, April 14, 1915 - Page 2

LOCALS

Mrs. Sallie D. Houk spent Friday night and Saturday with her sister, Mrs S.A.Maples of Cattlettsburg.

Mrs. H. C. Butler fell Sunday morning and suffered a broken arm. Dr. Massey was summoned and set the bones and her friends hope she may soon be well.

A son of George McKinley who lives near Montvale Springs crossing over the smoky mountains during the recent snow storm was found a few days ago by Riley Brackens of this county just across the state line frozen to death.

F. W. Sherrill, of the Johnson City State Normal School, has been named as State Superintendent of Public Instruction.

Questions

The notice in *MONTGOMERY'S VINDICATOR* seemed to shout that Edward McKinley's identity had not been a mystery for 60 years.

Here was the notice in a public newspaper, which had been published in a town about 20 miles from the Sugarlands community only twelve days after he was found. Before this conclusion could become a fact, several questions had to be answered.

Did two boys freeze to death on Deep Creek during Easter weekend in 1915?

The best evidence is that only one boy was found frozen to death on Easter weekend in 1915.

Was Edward McKinley's father named George?

Everything written prior to 1975 contained no names because the boy's identity was still a mystery. We checked everything Carson Brewer had written about Edward McKinley, and the names of the parents were not there. We called him. He recalled not including the names of Edward's parents, did not know the names and suggested we contact Lucinda Ogle. Mr. Brewer did not know about the MONTGOMERY'S VINDICATOR article.

It took weeks, but we did determine that Edward McKinley's father's name was George and that the family lived near Montvale Springs in Tennessee.

We had chanced upon a mystery within a mystery. We knew our chances of finding out how Edward's identity remained a mystery for over 60 years, when his father's name and location had been published in a newspaper, were slim to none. But read on!

We spoke with everyone we could find who knew about the unidentified boy found frozen to death on Deep Creek and buried in the Sugarlands, asking if they had ever seen or heard about the article in *MONTGOMERY'S VINDICATOR*. No one had. Even after we showed them a copy of the newspaper, they found it almost impossible to believe.

One of these persons was Lucinda Ogle. She said if her husband Earnest were alive, he would be dumbfounded. To learn that someone knew the identity of the boy, had it put in a newspaper, but had not told the people in the Sugarlands was a shock.

Betty Boone Best, a great niece of Edward McKinley, had written an article about him in 1985, which was published in the Winter 1985 newsletter of the Smoky Mountain Historical Society. She was very surprised to learn about the article.

How Could This Happen?

For those of us living in an age of instant communication and fast, comfortable transportation it is difficult to comprehend how this could have happened. There may be those who doubt it did happen, but the evidence that it did is overwhelming.

To begin to comprehend how this could happen, we must go back in time and look at the Sugarlands in 1915.

The Sugarlands community was light years away from what mountain communities are today. It was an isolated enclave within steep and heavily-forested mountains. The winters were severe.

There was no electricity, no telephones, no radios, no television, no automobiles, not even any bicycles. Travel was by foot, horseback or wagon. It was physically demanding and dangerous. Communication was mainly by word of mouth. Those who did leave the Sugarlands community were expected to learn what was happening and tell it when they returned home. Passersby were counted upon to bring and send word.

Mail was delivered to a central post office about twice a month during the summer and once a month during the winter. Everyone went the post office to 'call' for their mail. Stamps were beyond the means of many persons.

Lucinda Ogle told us that there were great numbers of persons who could not read and, consequently, had no need for newspapers. Many of those who could read were too poor to pay the price of a subscription to a newspaper, plus the expense of having it mailed to them.

The chances of the Edward McKinley mystery occurring in 1998 are infinitesimal. But, given the isolation, and certain human relationships within the Sugarlands community, it did occur.

Who Put the Notice in the Newspaper?

Someone knew the identity of the boy found frozen to death in Deep Creek and told the newspaper. But who was that someone? Was it Riley Brackens, the person reported to have found the son of George McKinley frozen to death just over the state line? Possibly. Or perhaps it was his brother, Davis Brackens.

Davis Brackens told Walter Diehl about the boy in June 1915. Walter Diehl was a source quoted by Carson Brewer in a follow-up story in *The Knoxville News-Sentinel* on August 3, 1975, that the mystery of the identity of the red-haired boy found frozen to death had been solved after 60 years.

If Riley Brackens was the source of the newspaper article, did he tell them he had found the boy or did the newspaper simply assume since he was making the report that he had?

How did he know the boy was the son of George McKinley who lived near Montvale Springs?

There is no definitive answer to these questions, but there is a very plausible explanation.

The boy who came to Goldie Brown's house told him he had stopped at another house down the road; but they had refused to let him stay. Since Riley and Davis Brackens were living in the cabin closest to Goldie Brown's cabin, Edward had probably stopped there. Or Edward might have encountered one or both of the Brackens on the trail and told them his name, his father's name, and where he lived.

There is no way to establish who supplied the information to *MONTGOMERY'S VINDICATOR*. It appears reasonable to conclude that it was either Riley or Davis Brackens or someone who knew them.

It is highly unlikely that any person who did not know Riley Brackens would have identified him as the person who found George McKinley's son frozen to death. This establishes the fact that the person supplying the information to *MONTGOMERY'S VINDICATOR* knew the name of the dead boy's father and where he lived. That person may have told George McKinley.

The story was published less than two weeks after he was found frozen to death. Why did the person who told the *MONTGOMERY'S VINDICATOR* about the boy not tell the persons who were sending word everywhere to try to identify him?

Riley Brackens may have seen this sad event as a way to help even the score with the Coles without doing any harm to the dead boy or his family.

To Even the Score?

Relations between Riley Brackens and the Cole clan were akin to the famed Hatfields and McCoys. Prior to 1915, Riley Brackens had killed three Cole boys.

Several Cole brothers, for reasons connected with moonshining, had sprayed bullets around Riley Brackens feet. They ordered him to 'dance to the bullets' or they would shoot him dead.

He danced, lived, and shot three of them dead in self-defense. The opportunity to even the score one again has come his way, just claim that he had found Edward.

Claiming that he, Riley Brackens, had found the boy would certainly provoke the Coles. If this is why Riley Brackens, and not the Cole cousins, was given credit for finding the boy, it was a dismal failure.

As far as anyone knows, the Cole cousins went to meet their maker without knowing the name of the boy they found on Deep Creek.

Those who knew them are positive if they had seen the article in *MONTGOMERY'S VINDICATOR* or heard that Riley Brackens was taking credit for snaking that dead boy over the mountains, they would have set the record straight with him.

Lasting Impressions

As we come to the end of the Edward McKinley story, three facts will always stay with us.

First and foremost, the people who found Edward McKinley, buried him, and remembered him through the years were kindhearted and generous. They cared for a stranger despite the hardships of their daily lives.

The second fact is a sad one. The mystery of the dead boy was foisted upon most of the people of the Sugarlands, by inexorable cirumstances in the time and place, or by persons who knew the truth but chose to conceal it.

And third, George McKinley caused heartache for his family by his edict that Edward's name could not be mentioned after he was dead.

Chapter 4
Edward (Edd) McKinley
Preface to Section C

We extend our appreciation to

Mrs. Hazel Newman Reagan
Dr. Robert Brackin Reed, Jr.
Mr. John Ownby
Mr. Carson Brewer
Mrs. Lucinda Oakley Ogle

for the information they provided about
Edward McKinley which is in this 2001 update.

~ ~

While researching the Edward McKinley story, we amassed much more material than we published. And the same is true of this update. We are publishing only what relates directly to Edward's story.

This necessary action in no way negates our enjoyment and appreciation of everything we have learned. We hope to hear from more readers before the next update of this book.

Chapter 4
Edward (Edd) McKinley
Section C

Shortly after *Unsolved Disappearances in the Great Smoky Mountains* went to the publisher, we learned from Mrs. Hazel Newman Reagan that Davis Brackens and Riley Brackens were not brothers but father and son.

Mrs. Reagan lived in the Smokies at the time Edward McKinley was found frozen to death. She knew the family well and recalls many happy times playing with the Brackens children.

After the book was published, Dr. Robert Brackin Reed, Jr. read it and contacted us. He is the great, great grandson of Riley Davis Brackin, Sr., and advised us that the correct spelling of the family name is "Brackin."

The records we had available contained many varied spellings of this name and we had opted for the "Brackens" because it appeared more than any other.

Edward's Fateful Decision

When this book was first published in 1998, we reported that Edward was on his way to his grandmother's home in Cherokee County, North Carolina. This is incorrect. His grandmother lived in Cherokee, North Carolina, which is in Swain County.

We also reported that Edward had told Goldie Brown that he had stopped at a house along the way but they had refused to let him in. That tugged at our heart strings and we found it hard to believe because such behavior was at odds with the behavior of the people in the area after he was found dead. We are happy to report that there is reliable information from Mrs. Hazel Newman Reagan and Dr. Robert Brackin Reed, Jr. that no one turned Edward away.

Mrs. Reagan remembers that Edward stopped at the home of one of her relatives, Bill Newman, in early afternoon. It was beginning to snow and they invited him to stay the night but he said he wanted to go on. After a short rest he went on his way.

Mrs. Reagan and Dr. Reed have information that later in the afternoon, Edward stopped at Riley Davis Brackin, Sr.'s home. Mr. Brackin was chopping wood and the children were carrying it into the house.

Edward was invited to eat supper and he accepted. After supper, Mr. Brackin told his children, and Edward, to bring in more wood because it was snowing hard and the night would be cold.

Edward is reported to have said, "No, if I have to do that I'll go on." And he did. That decision sealed his date with destiny.

Riley, Sr. tried to persuade him not to try to cross the Smokies in the snow storm. But Edward was determined to go. Before he left, Mr. Brackin told him about a cabin close to his route where he might need to seek shelter.

Who Found Edward McKinley's Body?

In all the sources we could locate before *Unsolved Disappearances in the Great Smoky Mountains* was first published, Jim and Joe Cole were credited with having found Edward's body quite by accident while on a hunting trip. However, Dr. Reed has different information. Ethyl Trentham told him that her father, Lev Trentham, a son-in-law of Riley Brackin, Sr., and Riley Brackin, Jr. found Edward McKinley.

Riley, Sr. was worried about him and sent Riley, Jr. and Lev Trentham to look for him because the night had been very cold and the storm had covered everything with several inches of snow.

She says they found him and dragged him back to the Brackin home.

* * * * *

Mr. John Ownby sent Juanitta Baldwin an e-mail stating: "My grandmother, Ethel Brackin, first told me back in the 60s of how her brother, Riley Brackin, and her brother-in-law, Lev Trentham, found the boy.

"She knew his name and where he was buried back then. She was 12 years old at the time of the incident but said she would never forget the sight of her brother carrying that boy's frozen body up to their house.

"She said he could still hear the strange howl of their dogs as they entered their front yard."

Juanitta Baldwin spoke with Mrs. Hazel Newman Reagan on several occasions about the information from Dr. Reed and Mr. Ownby that Lev Trentham and Riley Brackin, Jr. found Edward McKinley. Mrs. Reagan found the information very puzzling and had no explanation for the difference in what she remembers and what Ethel Brackin, Mr. Ownby's grandmother, told him. She said none of the Brackin children ever mentioned seeing Edward after he refused to carry in wood and left their house in the snow.

She said, "It seems logical that members of the Newman and Brackin families learned Edward McKinley's name when he stopped at their homes. If any of them told anyone involving in burying him, it was forgotten. He was buried as the *little boy known only to God.* I never heard his name until I read the story about his sister coming to the Park to look for him.

"Earnest Ogle helped dig the grave. He told me that when saw the boy his clothes had been cut by the Coles and used to tie him to a lizard they'd made on the spot, and how hard it had been for them to drag him from Deep Creek to the Sugarlands."

* * * * *

Juanitta also spoke with Mrs. Lucinda Oakley Ogle about the information that Lev Trentham and Riley, Jr. found Edward. "I am positive that the Coles found Edward McKinley because my husband, Earnest lived in the Sugarlands and helped dig the grave to bury him. I wrote all the details he told me to the Park service way back about 1970."

Dr. Reed has not been able to obtain specifics as to who moved Edward's body from the Brackin home to the Sugarlands for burial in the Sugarlands Cemetery.

He speculates that it a reasonable possibility that the

Coles came into the picture either by Lev Trentham and Riley, Jr. chancing upon them during their search, or after the body was brought to the Brackin home. The Brackin home was higher up in the Smokies than the Sugarlands, so after Lev and Riley, Jr. dragged the body to Riley, Sr.'s home, the Coles could have dragged it on down to the Sugarlands.

As to the matter of Edward's name, he believes the Brackin family may have mentioned it to people and that it could have easily been forgotten by everyone. There is the possibility that someone remembered and that is how the notice of Edward's death came to be published in *MONTGOMERY'S VINDICATOR.*

* * * * *

Juanitta e-mailed Mr. Ownby and asked if he had specifics as to how the body was moved to the Sugarlands, or why Edward was buried as an unknown. Mr. Ownby did not reply.

* * * * *

Juanitta spoke with Mr. Carson Brewer about the report that Lev and Riley, Jr. found Edward McKinley.

He said all his information identified the Cole cousins as the persons who found Edward. The only thing he learned about Davis Braken (Riley Davis Brackin, Sr.) while writing about Edward was from a Captain Walter Diehl in response to a query. He learned that Captain Diehl, who was a student at the University of Tennessee in 1915, had spent Easter weekend camping in the Smokies with a group of students from the Botany Department. Captain Diehl wrote, "On my next trip, about the middle of June 1915, I was told by Davis Bracken (Riley Davis Brackin, Sr. used the name Davis) of the boy who froze to death not more than one-half mile from our camp. We had seen signs of footprints on our way to Indian Gap."

At that time Mr. Brewer had no information that there was a question about who found Edward and did not question Captain Diehl on that point.

* * * * *

Who found Edward is an intriguing point in this story, but it may never be resolved.

It does not change the basic story of a determined young man who tempted fate and lost. Nor does it change the fact that whoever found him, and other residents in the Smokies, were kind and cared enough to bury him among their own.

So, respected readers, you decide! We have reported everything but cannot solve the riddle. Perhaps someone has more information?

Who Made the Report to the Newspaper?

The stops Edward made at the Newman and Brackin homes offer a plausible explanation of how someone knew his name to report it to the newspaper, *MONTGOMERY'S VINDICATOR*. It was probably a Newman or a Brackin.

This, coupled with the new information that Lev Trentham and Riley, Jr. may have found Edward, calls the theory that Riley, Jr. may have told the newspaper that he found Edward to even the score with the Coles into question. Dr. Reed, having explored his heritage, says with certainty that, "Riley, Jr. would not have resorted to taking credit for something in a newspaper to get back at someone. That was too passive for him. He would have handled a dispute face to face.

"Riley, Sr. shot two Newman brothers in self-defense because they were blaming Riley, Jr. for the death of a third Newman brother in World War I."

Dr. Reed does not have any information about Riley, Sr. having shot any Cole brothers to death, only two Newman brothers.

Mrs. Reagan says she distinctly remembers that Riley, Sr. shot two Newmans and Amos Cole.

Mrs. Ogle told Juanitta several times that she has heard the story all her life about the Coles making Riley, Sr. dance to bullets and his shooting them later on.

Whatever the precise facts as to what the Coles did to Riley, Sr., or who Riley, Sr. shot, it appears that the shootings can be discounted as a motive for making a report to *MONTGOMERY'S VINDICATOR*.

Still a Puzzler

As we came to the end of the 2001 update of the Edward McKinley story, the mystery of how he could have been buried as an unidentified boy, *known only to God*, remained unsolved. And it remains a mystery in 2009.

Chapter 5
Abe Carroll Ramsey

March 11, 1919, began as an ordinary Monday for the Ramsey family. Their three-room cabin stood beside Dunns Creek in the Great Smoky Mountains in Tennessee. But this would not be an ordinary Monday. Three-year-old Abe Carroll Ramsey would disappear.

* * * * *

As a thin band of pink-orange light silhouetted the steep, heavily-forested mountains ringing their isolated cabin, John and Mary Jane Ramsey slept peacefully in one of the three double beds in the big room.

Clyda 6 months, Abe Carroll 3, and Joe 6, were in the bed closest to the fireplace. Ola 14, and Ruthie 12, were in the third bed.

The sun rolled over the mountains like a huge silver ball, and within minutes the day was bright and brittle. Tattered and faded patchwork quilts hung over the windows to stop the cold kept the cabin in deep twilight.

Clyda was the first to wake. She wiggled and cooed with tiny grunts but did not cry. Perhaps she was soothed by the melodic lullaby of water trickling across the rocky bottom of Dunns Creek and the faint tinkling of a cow bell.

Mary Jane awoke and smiled as she heard Clyda,

feeling thankful she was not given to squalling. Maybe the thin beams of sunlight seeping through the gaps between the quilts and the windows might mean the Good Lord had heard her plea for a fit wash day.

Mary Jane sat up and pulled her dress on over her flowered, flannel petticoat. Her shivers shook the bed as she pulled on heavy cotton stockings and brogans. John, 41, whom she cherished as a good-provider husband, was lying on his back snoring loud enough to wake the dead. She suspected he played possum until she had fire roaring in the fireplace and in the cook stove.

She never let on about John playing possum. She liked to change Clyda, nurse her, and put her back to bed without him and their younguns clambering about.

An Ordinary Day

Warm air, wafting the scent of sizzling fat back, brought John and the younguns to life. They ringed the hearth to wash their hands and faces with rags they dipped into a galvanized pan Ola had filled with water and placed on the hearth last night. This done, everyone took their usual seat at the table.

There was little conversation until the bowls brimming with fried fatback, corn meal mush and buttermilk biscuits were empty.

John looked out the window. "Looks like a purty decent day. Don't you younguns lollygag after school lets out. Remember to carry in water and wood."

Abe stood on the porch beside Motley, the family's

giant rawboned hound, and chanted, "Bye, bye," as John left for the mill and his siblings for school.

Abe grinned happily and continued his "bye, bye" singsong until Mary Jane came out on the porch with a tin plate of food for Motley. Abe reached for it. Motley whooshed between them, tipped the plate and scattered the corn pone and fatback scraps across the porch. She sighed but said nothing. Motley would find, and devour, every morsel.

Mary Jane shielded her eyes from the bright sunlight and peered east toward the mill. John stopped to open the cap on the millrace to start the huge waterwheel turning.

This meant John was going to grind corn before he went up the mountainside to the moonshine still where he helped make whiskey. He always ground enough corn meal to fool 'the law' if they came snooping around. She did not mind John working at the still but did worry that he might be arrested.

The mill was owned by their closest neighbor whose farm was about a mile away. The same neighbor owned the still. If John did not work at the still, he would lose his job at the mill. Making whiskey, commonly referred to as 'moonshine,' was against the law. Compliance with 'that tomfoolery' was for the fainthearted. The local sheriff could usually be kept away by 'pictures of George Washington in a firm handshake.'

Federal 'lawmen' were a threat, but most of them were outsiders and did not know mountain ways. Only once in a blue moon were they able to sneak up undetected and raid a still. Moonshiners took rifles with them to their stills. They knew how to shoot and shot when they thought their still was threatened.

What John earned at the mill, and at the still, was a godsend. Their rough farm, of about a hundred acres, had less than ten acres of tillable soil; and it was poor. In good weather years, they managed to grow enough vegetables to feed the family. They raised pigs for meat and kept several cows for milk and butter.

* * * * *

After looking in on Clyda, who was sleeping soundly, Mary Jane went into the yard to wash. She washed all morning, stopping occasionally to check on Clyda. Abe watched the fire under the boiling pot. The moment a stick burned he replaced it until she said, "I'm about done, Sugar. Let the fire die, and we'll eat."

Motley heard dogs barking on the mountain and streaked off to investigate. Hunters, probably. Sometimes 'the law' brought dogs with them when they were looking for a still. Mary Jane heard an explosion of muffled barks. Motley had encountered dogs and was probably in a fight.

About three o'clock, she helped Abe into his coat. He pulled his toboggan on, taking great pride in doing something all by himself. She slipped on a heavy jacket and went to check to see if the wash was dry.

Surprisingly, Motley had not returned; and Abe ran around the yard, then toward the creek, looking for him.

"Come back," Mary Jane called.

Abe ran to the clothesline, trying to catch the clothes flapping like kites in the brisk March wind. Mary Jane took an arm load of clothes into the house.

"Abe," she called from the porch, "come here."

There was no answer, and Abe was nowhere in sight. She felt something was wrong. After a quick look inside to be certain he had not gone into the back room, she circled the house, looked in the privy, and under the house. No sign of Abe.

Motley was whimpering under the porch. She bent down and saw he had been in a fight. There was no time to see about him now.

"Abe, if yer hidin', come out this minute."

Silence.

She ran to the creek bank. No tracks except her own. Hoping he had gone to the mill, she raced to it as fast as she could. No one was there. Abe's tracks were not by the millrace.

Back at the house, she looked under every bed, behind the cook stove and under the eating table. She searched as far into the woods as she could and still keep an eye on the house and yard. Clyda was inside, and she hoped desperately to see Abe walk into view.

The children came home from school about an hour after Abe disappeared. She sent Ola to tell the neighbors that Abe was missing and ask anyone who could to come and help hunt for him.

She left Ruthie and Joe to watch Clyda while she sprinted up the mountainside to the still. John did not want the younguns to know where the still was for fear they would tell outsiders. The still was deserted. She looked on each side of the path as she made her way back to their cabin and called Abe's name.

Ola returned with two neighbors who had come to help. John came home shortly thereafter. He looked dazed and said he had heard the news before he came home. He had been at the general store owned by his brother, Lloyd Ramsey, and someone had come in to spread the word about Abe.

Mary Jane knew why he had been at the store and not at the still. Lloyd Ramsey sold the supplies moonshiners needed and sold moonshine for them.

Word that little Abe Ramsey was missing spread quickly. Several neighbors and their dogs searched most of the night. John sat on the steps and wept, declaring he was 'jest too tore up to take part.'

While the search was going on, John had a private talk with Mary Jane. The hope went out of her eyes. She sat silently as he told Abe's siblings that some crazy or wicked man had watched until he got the chance to steal Abe.

That wicked man had wanted Abe for his own because he was a bright child, with promise of growing up able and strong. John publically vowed to track him down and shoot him in cold blood.

No one found any trace of Abe that night.

Abe Must be Found

By the next day, word that Abe Ramsey was lost, and must be found quickly because of the cold weather, spread across Cocke county. Family, neighbors and strangers searched the mountainsides surrounding the cabin. Dunns Creek was searched for miles.

For the next three days, they searched more ground in every direction than it was reasonable to think little Abe could have walked or crawled.

After four days and no trace of Abe had been found the search ended. Family members and neighbors had work to be done. In 1919, there were no search teams, no rescue squads, and no easy way for willing volunteers to come from far and wide.

It was a hard truth to face, but Abe Ramsey was lost. Perhaps forever.

Life After Abe Disappeared

Inexplicably the still where John had worked the day Abe disappeared was destroyed, and all signs of it erased.

It had not been found by 'the law.' Moonshiners moved their stills often as a precaution so this did not raise many questions in the close circle that knew its location until later in the summer.

* * * * *

John Ramsey lettered signs with a tar mixture on wood offering a $100 reward for information to help him find his lost child. He nailed them to trees along every trail and road for miles around.

No one ever tried to claim the reward.

As the weeks past, most of the mountain folks were persuaded that Abe had either drowned or been attacked and devoured by some type of wild animal. Few gave any credence to the notion Abe had been kidnapped.

No strangers had been spotted in the mountains at the time Abe disappeared.

To the untrained eye, the mountains in Cocke County appeared devoid of human surveillance, but not so. In 1919, Cocke County was the Moonshine Capital of the United States. It was essential to know who was about at all times.

The conventional wisdom was that a would-be kidnapper would find a more convenient place to steal a child. Three-year-old Abe could not walk out of the rugged mountains. Carrying Abe and basic supplies would be difficult even for a strong man.

* * * * *

John did resume work at the mill, and eventually he worked at other stills. However, for the rest of his life he was considered to be 'poorly.'

He talked about Abe to anyone who would listen, trying to convince them he had been kidnapped. He asked every person from another location with whom he came in contact to look for him. Only one lead was ever developed.

In September 1919, word came that a man, half-Indian and half-Negro, had been seen near Soco Gap in North Carolina, fifty some miles away, with a white child about Abe's age.

John told everyone he was going to Soco Gap to look for Abe. When he returned, he said the man and the child had moved by the time he got there. He was gone such a short time that few people believed he could have made the long, hard trip to Soco Gap and back.

Three Tales About What Happened to Abe

By late summer 1919, three tales about what really happened to Abe Carroll Ramsey were being whispered in the Dunns Creek community among those who could be trusted with secrets.

By Christmas the tales became secrets almost everyone in Cocke County, and adjacent Sevier County, knew.

The three tales appear to have originated with moonshiners. They told what had really happened to little Abe Ramsey 'in absolute confidence' to persons they trusted. Their secret burden was too heavy to carry alone.

In each of the three tales, what happened to Abe took place at a moonshine still on a mountain close to the Ramsey cabin. Each tale has a different version of what happened at that moonshine still.

Tale One

On the day Abe "wandered away" there were several barrels of mash fermenting at the still. The barrels were buried in the ground and camouflaged with brush to hide them from rogues and "the law."

When the moonshiners came to check on the mash they found Abe in a barrel of mash. He had fallen into the barrel and drowned. Horrified, and terrified, they made a pact to carry this secret with them to their graves.

One man went to his home and got a big suitcase to use as a coffin. They dug a deep grave in a laurel thicket, buried Abe, and camouflaged his grave by pouring water over the fresh earth and piling it high with brush.

John Ramsey was one of the moonshiners at the still the day Abe was discovered. He told Mary Jane but no one else for a long, long time. They agreed to pretend Abe had been kidnapped because they feared that John, his brother Lloyd and others would be arrested for moonshining.

After a time, there was no reason to tell what had really happened. Nothing would bring Abe back. Their grief was deep and real beneath the facade of pretense, made even more painful because they had feared to tell the truth for so many years.

In their last years, John and Mary Jane Ramsey dropped the pretense that Abe had been kidnapped when talking with family and those they trusted.

Tale Two

Abe "wandered up" the mountain where John and several other moonshiners were at work. They heard limbs cracking and at first assumed it was a wild animal. When the sounds continued, it sounded like "the law" trying to slip up to make a raid.

A yell went out for the password or signal. When there was no response two or three men fired their rifles, then went to investigate.

Little Abe Ramsey lay mortally wounded. Horrified, and terrified, they carried him out of the woods. He died within minutes. John Ramsey was distraught but realized if the truth was told he and the others at the still would be arrested. Making whiskey at this still was how they made money to feed their families, and John had other children to feed.

The moonshiners made a pact to carry this terrible secret to their graves. One man went home and got a big suitcase. They dug a deep grave in a laurel thicket, buried him, and camouflaged his grave.

As the last surviving moonshiner who had been at the still when Abe was shot lay on his deathbed, he called a trusted relative to his bedside and told his version of what had happened to Abe Ramsey.

He said he could not meet his maker without confessing he had shot Abe Ramsey. Although several men had fired shots that day, he said he was the only one who saw the bullet that killed Abe. The bullet was from his rifle.

It was his dying wish that the real truth be told to all the members of Abe's family who were still alive.

The deathbed wish was carried out. This tale, which had circulated for years, was confirmed as fact in the minds of those who had heard it and believed it.

Tale Three

The third tale is perhaps the most heart wrenching of all. It is identical to the second one, except that John Ramsey fired the fatal shot.

Part III
Deliberate Disappearances

William Bradford Bishop, Jr., indicted for murdering his family disappeared in 1976. He is a notorious fugitive believed to have eluded capture by disappearing into the Smokies in 1976. It is now 1998. He has not been found alive or dead.

* * * * *

Eric Robert Rudolph, a bombing suspect, disappeared in January 1998. He is a suspect in the bombing of an abortion clinic in Birmingham, Alabama. As this book goes to press in September 1998, he is still at large.

* * * * *

The Great Smoky Mountains are covered with thick growths of trees and bushes. There are deep valleys, caves and hundreds of places to hide.

Fugitives flee into the Smokies to elude capture. Most are inexperienced and do not fare well. They are usually caught in a short time or surface on their own to escape death. Fugitives who know how to survive in the mountains stay in them longer.

Some fugitives do not survive. Others choose to end their own lives before they are captured. In both of these instances, the bodies are usually found.

Chapter 6
William Bradford Bishop, Jr.

On Thursday, March 18, 1976, Roy Ownby saw a bronze 1974 Chevrolet station wagon in a secluded gravel parking lot at Elkmont in Great Smoky Mountains National Park. It was dirty, littered with broken twigs and appeared to have been abandoned. Mr. Ownby called Park Headquarters, and a Park ranger came to inspect.

The station wagon was locked. A check for keys possibly hidden in the undercarriage was made. None were found. The license plates were traced to William Bradford Bishop, Jr. 39, of Bethesda, Maryland, through the National Crime Information Center.

The Park ranger learned that an all points police bulletin had been issued in Bethesda on March 8, 1976, asking for assistance in locating Bradford Bishop. Police wanted to question him about the murders of his wife, their three sons and his mother on March 1, 1976.

The locked station wagon was towed to Park Headquarters. FBI agents arrived to inspect it. More FBI agents, state troopers and park rangers converged on the area immediately to search for Bradford Bishop.

A small army of reporters from local and national media arrived. They were not allowed to accompany the searchers, but they were relentless in ferreting out every detail of the search. News coverage about what was happening was immediate and worldwide.

Park rangers concluded that the station wagon had been in the parking lot for about two weeks. One reason it was not noticed immediately is because the parking lot where it was found is used by Park visitors and residents of the old lumbering town of Elkmont, one of the few private land areas which remained within the Park boundaries.

There were about 30 structures in Elkmont in 1976, scattered along a network of hiking trails leading from the unpaved parking lot. The homes were used mainly for vacations, and most were empty most of the time. There was no formal checking system for vehicles. No one saw who parked the station wagon.

Evidence was developed very quickly that Bradford Bishop drove it there. Three main trails lead into the Park from this parking lot. All of them connect with other trails in the wilderness.

This makes it an attractive place for a fugitive to go into the Smokies on foot.

William B. Bishop Jr.

Who is William Bradford Bishop, Jr.?

Bradford Bishop was employed by the U. S. State Department in Washington, DC, as an economic affairs officer specializing in commerce treaties. He had gone into government service shortly after he earned a master's degree in African studies from Yale University, and had become proficient in several languages.

He had served tours of duty in Africa, Ethiopia, Italy and Botswana; and his family had accompanied him. The family apparently made friends everywhere they lived. They were well known and well liked in State Department circles.

Although Bradford Bishop's superiors regarded him as a seasoned professional, the competition for promotion within the State Department was formidable. He was bitterly disappointed when he was not selected for promotion in mid-February 1976.

Several coworkers repeated conversations with him in which he had told them that his wife would think him a failure and make life miserable for him.

Mr. Bishop's superiors said they had observed that he had seemed anxious, irritable and depressed during most of February 1976. He told one superior he had consulted a psychiatrist and was taking the antidepressant drug Serax, and it seemed to alleviate his condition.

During the last week of February, Bradford Bishop had exhibited symptoms of a cold. On March 1, 1976, he called in sick, stating he was suffering from influenza and would probably be absent several days.

The Bradford Bishop Family

Until March 1, 1976, Bradford Bishop lived with his wife, Annette 37; sons William Bradford III, 14; Brenton 10; Geoffrey 5; his mother Lovellia Bishop 68; and Leo, their golden retriever, in an upscale suburban neighborhood in Bethesda, Maryland.

The Bishop home was in the $100,000 price range, with a large, manicured front lawn. The back yard, shaded by large trees and fenced, provided safe play space for the children and Leo.

The Bishops were well-known and well-liked by their neighbors. William Bradford, III, and Brenton attended a local school. Both were considered good students.

Residents in the neighborhood knew the general routines of one another, and there was an informal community watch to guard against robbery and crime.

Most neighbors knew Bishop held a high stress job with the State Department. Only a few knew he was undergoing treatment for alcoholism or that he was being treated by a psychiatrist for severe depression. Most of his coworkers, neighbors and friends knew Bishop to be a skilled and avid outdoorsman and camper.

The Bishop Family Disappeared

The Bradford Bishop family and Leo were last seen on March 1, 1976.

Several neighbors became concerned after not seeing anyone, or any activity in or around the home, for five days. They noticed the lights in two rooms upstairs had been on all night for several nights. There was no normal switching

on and off of lights in and around the home after March 1,
1976. No one answered the repeated ringing of the door-
bell and knocks on the door. Several neighbors called the
home telephone number many times. There was no answer.

William Bradford III, and Brenton Bishop were not in
school, and there had been no notification they would be
absent. Normally if either boy was to be absent, Mrs.
Bishop made it a point to explain why he would be absent.

The Bishops usually told neighbors and friends when
they would be away, but no member of the family had
mentioned any travel plans. On March 6, 1976, two
neighbors became so concerned they notified the Bethesda,
Maryland, Police Department. Police officers went to the
home. All the doors and windows were locked. They did
not get a response.

Nothing seemed suspicious except that mail had accu-
mulated in the mailbox for several days. A check with the
local post office was made. The Bishops had not followed
their usual procedure of asking that their mail be held while
they were away. The police determined that a search of the
house should be made.

A Chilling Discovery

Police found blood in several rooms, upstairs and
downstairs, but there were no bodies. Also a massive
amount of blood was smeared across the floors, as if a
body, or bodies, had been dragged.

Most of the blood had dried, indicating that it had been
there several days. There were no signs of a struggle or of a

gun having been fired in the home. The only weapon found was a bloody baseball bat.

The neighbors were stunned. The police questioned everyone who lived in the neighborhood, or was known to have been in it, since the first of March. No one had seen or heard anything unusual at the residence. No one at the State Department had heard from Bradford Bishop after his call on March 1, 1976.

Those who knew the Bishops best were at a loss to offer any possible motive why anyone would want to murder them. For a time, the neighbors feared Bradford Bishop had been killed along with his family and Leo.

Finding the Bishop Family

The police were faced with finding out why there was so much blood in the Bishop residence and where the Bishops had gone.

The logical conclusion was that the blood would be found to belong to one or more members of the Bishop family. And possibly to Leo.

Within a few hours, they learned where everyone except Bradford Bishop and Leo had gone.

Five Bodies Found in North Carolina

Police Departments all over the United States had received a bulletin on March 2, 1976, asking for help in identifying five bodies which had been found in a remote pine forest in Tyrell County in eastern North Carolina about twenty miles from the small town of Columbia.

A forest ranger in a fire watchtower had spotted smoke and had driven to investigate. He had found bodies burning

in an open, gasoline-soaked pit. The ranger summoned
help, and the fire was extinguished. After the pit cooled, the
authorities determined there were five badly charred bodies
in it, two adults and three children.

The bodies were examined and it was determined that
each person had been bludgeoned to death with a blunt
object before being dumped in the shallow pit, doused with
gasoline, and set on fire. The fire officials believed the fire
was of such intensity it would have destroyed the bodies
beyond identification if it had not been spotted as quickly as
it was.

There was nothing at the site to identify any of the
bodies. The only object found was a long-handled shovel.

By March 8, 1976, the shovel had been traced to a
Potomac, Maryland, hardware store. The shovel had been
paid for with cash, and no one at the store could recall who
had purchased it.

A bulletin about it was sent to all police departments in
the country on March 8, 1976. The police in Montgomery
County had searched the Bishop home, so an immediate
connection was made between the shovel and bodies in
North Carolina.

Armed with the information about the murders in
Bethesda, Maryland, the bodies in North Carolina were
identified very quickly as Bradford Bishop's wife, mother,
and three sons.

The fact Bradford Bishop's body was not among the
victims conclusively ruled out any other person as the

murder suspect. Shock and disbelief were the immediate reactions of the Bishops' neighbors and friends and those who knew Bradford Bishop at the State Department. No one had seen any warning signs. The most puzzling aspect of the case was still the lack of any known or suspected motive for the killings.

Tracking Bradford Bishop

No one had seen the person or persons who brought the bodies to the spot in the pine forest in Tyrell County, North Carolina. No one had seen who had tried to burn them, but the evidence for both these crimes pointed to Bradford Bishop.

A credit card belonging to Bishop had been used at a Jacksonville, North Carolina, sporting goods store on March 2, 1976, for $15.60 worth of items described on the charge slip as outdoor supplies. The supplies were not itemized. Handwriting experts positively identified the signature on the credit card slip as Bradford Bishop's. This placed him in North Carolina the day after he was believed to have murdered his family.

When the station wagon found in the Smokies was inspected, there was conclusive evidence that it had been used to transport the bodies of Bishop's family from Maryland to North Carolina. The rear of the wagon was covered by two very large canvas tarpaulins, and the underside of each was spattered with blood. Beneath them were several blood soaked blankets, and the entire flat surface in the rear of the station wagon was smeared with blood.

Leo had not been seen since the first of March, the last day any of the Bishop family was seen by neighbors. He could have been with Mr. Bishop when he parked the station wagon, or he could have been put out anywhere along the long trip from Bethesda to Tyrell County, North Carolina, where the bodies were found, or on the drive to the Smoky Mountains. There was a box of dog biscuits on the floor on the passenger side of the wagon, and dog biscuit crumbs across the front seat.

Inspectors inventoried the other items in the station wagon:

one loaded 12 gauge shotgun in a case, with additional ammunition,

a man's top coat and other clothing,

one suitcase containing men's clothing and personal items,

one long-handled axe with blood on the handle,

several containers of medicine,

maps of Atlanta and Miami,

a credit card receipt from a service station near Columbia, North Carolina,

and camping equipment.

Knowing Bishop was a skilled camper, the authorities knew he could survive in the Smoky Mountain wilderness longer than an unskilled person.

They assumed he had taken some camping equipment with him when he fled into the mountains. They conjectured his plan might have been to hike through the Smokies to a public road where he could escape without leaving a trail. He would probably camp as necessary to survive and elude capture. The manhunt was on worldwide.

Searching the Smokies for Bradford Bishop

Twenty-five FBI agents, two FBI dog handlers with bloodhounds and 22 Park rangers assembled to search for Bishop. They fanned out from the parking lot where Bishop's station wagon had been found.

Moments after the search began, a bloodhound named J. Edgar went straight to the door of the cabin nearest to where the station wagon had been parked. J. Edgar refused to leave until searchers took him inside the cabin. They found no evidence that Bradford Bishop had been inside the cabin, but they were confident he had been on the steps and porch.

All the structures in Elkmont were thoroughly searched with totally negative results.

Roads in and out of the area were closed to the public during the search, and no camping or back packing permits were issued. Campers and back packers who were in the search area were questioned.

A group of Explorer Scouts from Nacogdoches, Texas, said they were hiking on March 18, 1976, and talked with a man and woman who identified themselves only as 'Mike and Betty' from Cleveland, Ohio. They told the Scouts they had camped the night before with a man wearing street clothes and carrying a tent in a duffle bag who said he was heading for Newfound Gap. FBI agents went to Newfound

Gap but did not find the 'Mike and Betty' or anyone hiking in street clothes.

Newspapers, radio and television quoted the FBI as describing Bradford Bishop as very dangerous and having possible suicidal tendencies, particularly so if he had not secured a refill for his antidepressant drug Serax. One possibility, the FBI said, was that he may have hiked up one of the trails and committed suicide. If he had, they wanted to find his body.

Doctors, pharmacists and hospitals across the country were alerted to watch for Bradford Bishop requesting a refill of his prescription for Serax.

After a frustrating three-and-a-half day search yielded no clues as to Bishop's whereabouts in the Smokies, the intensive search ended.

In the year after Bradford Bishop's trail ended in the Great Smoky Mountains National Park, FBI agents interviewed over 1200 people who had camped or hiked there after his station wagon was found. Several of these persons believed they had encountered Bradford Bishop but no contact could be confirmed.

Bradford Bishop Indicted for Murder

On March 20, 1976, a grand jury in Montgomery County, Maryland, indicted William Bradford Bishop, Jr. on five counts of murder. He was charged with the bludgeoning deaths of his wife, their three sons and his mother. Police had no clue as to his whereabouts and had not developed any motive for the murders.

The Worldwide Search

Five months after William Bradford Bishop, Jr., left his office never to return, the State Department terminated his employment. The working assumption at the State Department was that he had left the country.

The FBI issued a statement it would have been extremely difficult for Bishop to disappear so successfully on his own after such a botched crime. They thought he probably had an accomplice. Another possibility was that he had obtained a forged passport well in advance. If this was the case, he had probably hiked out of the Smokies within a few days after the station wagon was abandoned and left the country.

The search for William Bradford Bishop, Jr., would be worldwide. The Bishop case generated worldwide publicity for several months.

Not one lead surfaced until 1978. There was a brief surge of excitement when a newspaper published a picture of hostages taken by Moluccan terrorists in the Netherlands. One of the hostages resembled Bishop. He turned out to be a Dutch taxi driver.

* * * * *

In the first week of July 1979, the FBI received a report that Bishop had been seen in Stockholm, Sweden.

A woman, who said she knew Bishop and his family in Ethiopia between 1965 and 1968, said Bishop wore a beard and, although she was positive she recognized him, made no attempt to speak with him.

Agents spent weeks searching for Bishop in the area where this woman had reported seeing him, but every possibility evaporated.

* * * * *

In October of 1979, Roy Harrell, a State Department employee who had served with Bishop, reported that he was almost positive he had come face to face with him in Sorrento, Italy. Harrell was in a public rest room when another man entered. He was startled and blurted out, "Say, aren't you Brad Bishop?"

Harrell said the man replied in English, "Oh, my God no," and ran out, disappearing into a blinding rain. A thorough investigation in Sorrento turned up nothing.

Unsolved Mysteries *Profiles Bishop*

The television program *Unsolved Mysteries* profiled the case of William Bradford Bishop, Jr., in 1980 and has shown it several times since. The producers of the show told us new information is received after each broadcast, and it will continue to be on the air periodically for sometime to come.

Bradford Bishop would turn 61 years old in 1998. He was not in the best of health when he disappeared. With proper medication, he may still be alive.

The Search for Bishop Continues

William Bradford Bishop, Jr., if alive, has eluded worldwide attempts to find him.

The case is still open as this book goes to press in 1998. The FBI told us it will remain open until Bishop, or his body, is found.

Chapter 7
Eric Robert Rudolph
2001 and 2006 Updates Follow

As this book goes to press in March 1999, the FBI is searching the Great Smoky Mountains for Eric Robert Rudolph. He is the prime suspect in the bombing of the New Woman All Women abortion clinic in Birmingham, Alabama, on January 29, 1998.

Emily Lyons, a nurse, was severely injured, and Birmingham police officer Sandy Sanderson was killed.

Eric Rudolph is also wanted for questioning in connection with the explosion in Centennial Park during the 1996 Olympics in Atlanta, Georgia.

Prior to becoming a fugitive in hiding, Eric Rudolph lived in Marble and near Andrews, North Carolina. After his father died while he was a teenager, his oldest brother, Daniel, took care of him. On March 8, 1998, Daniel purposely cut off one of his hands with an electric saw. He videotaped the amputation, recording on the tape, "This is being done to send a message to the FBI and the media."

Authorities know Eric Rudolph is skilled in mountain survival. He has eluded the hundreds of troops that have searched for him on the ground and successfully hidden from the technical devices utilized in helicopters and planes to detect a human body.

A million dollar reward has been offered by the FBI. It has not flushed him out. Will Eric Rudolph be another William Bradford Bishop, Jr.?

2001 Update on Eric Robert Rudolph

The T-shirts admonishing "Run Rudolph Run" are faded now, and the bumper stickers dubbing him "World Hide and Seek Champion" are peeling, but the hunt, which has cost over $15 million, goes on.

Robert Eric Rudolph is on the FBI's 10 Most Wanted Fugitive List, and there is $1,000,000 reward for information leading directly to his arrest.

The FBI poster carries the warning that Rudolph is to be considered armed and extremely dangerous.

Authorities are confident he is hiding in Nantahala Forest near Andrews, North Carolina. He grew up exploring this dark forest, dense with rattlesnakes, wild boar, towering hardwoods, and hundreds of caves and abandoned mica and copper mines.

From the beginning, residents and community leaders have been divided over who deserves their support: Rudolph or law enforcement personnel. Some members of the clergy urge their members to volunteer any information they have; others say they think Rudolph deserves support for bombing an abortion clinic since they believe that abortion is murder and should be stopped by any means.

Former Cherokee County Sheriff Jack Thompson does not out rule the possibility that Rudolph is being aided by locals. He still remembers every detail of the day he and federal agents came within minutes of capturing Rudolph.

They went to Rudolph's trailer, at the end of a dirt road on an isolated mountain. The door was wide open, fresh food on the table, CNN blaring from the television, and signs that Rudolph had fled, probably into the nearby woods.

In August 1998, former Green Beret Colonel James "Bo" Gritz led a band of 40 unarmed volunteers to bring Rudolph out of the woods so he could surrender safely. The search was futile.

Authorities have encountered stronger sentiment for Rudolph than just words from pulpits, T-shirts and bumper stickers.

In 1998, slugs from a high-powered rifle pierced the walls of the search headquarters, and parted the hair of an FBI agent. No one has ever been apprehended for this shooting.

During 1999, several mountain homes were broken into. Food, toilet paper, and similar supplies were stolen. In some instances the intruder took a shower and shaved. Authorities suspected Rudolph was the culprit. The break-ins ceased and this reinforced the speculation that residents are helping him to survive and elude capture.

In June 2000, the FBI began recruiting locals who are familiar with the remote mountains to scout for Rudolph. They are paid $15 to $20 and hour to scale the peaks and listen. So far there have been no results. Many are openly amused, or cynical, and deride using locals as turning the fox into the hen house.

If Rudolph is hiding in the mountains, he may die from the cold, at the hand of a disgruntled supporter, associate, bounty hunter, or from his own paranoia. If this happens, the questions about what he really did will never be answered, and his disappearance may remain unsolved forever.

2006 Update on Eric Robert Rudolph

Rudolph was captured in Murphy, North Carolina, at 4:30 AM on May 31, 2003, by a Sheriff's Deputy who saw him pilfering through a dumpster behind a grocery store. Rudolph surrendered without any resistance.

Rudolph's capture ended his status as an almost mythical figure to fellow radicals everywhere. Although none of the locals that Juanitta Baldwin interviewed from the date he disappeared until after his sentencing would admit to aiding Rudolph, several refused to deny it. One minister told her that God was on the side all who helped him.

In 2005, Rudolph struck a plea deal that spared him the death penalty, but ensured he will spend the rest of his life in prison. He apologized to his victims and their families for his 1996 bombing of Centennial Olympic Park, but did not apologize for any of his other attacks.

Rudolph is in the United States Penitentiary Administrative Maximum Facility in Florence, Colorado. He sports #18282-058 on his garments. Like other inmates, he spends 23 hours per day in his concrete cell instead of roaming the Great Smoky Mountains.

Bibliography

The documentary references listed here were used in researching this book. Those with an asterisk beside the name have ceased publication.

Newspapers

* *MONTGOMERY'S VINDICATOR,* Sevierville, Tennessee, may be viewed on microfilm at the Sevier County Library, 321 Court Avenue, Sevierville, Tennessee 37862.

* *The Gatlinburg Press*, 1967, Gatlinburg, Tennessee

The Knoxville Journal may be viewed on microfilm at Lawson-McGhee Library, 500 West Church Street, Knoxville, Tennessee 37902.

* *Smoky Mountain Star*, Pigeon Forge, Tennessee

* *Sevier County Times*, Sevierville, Tennessee

The Mountain Press, Sevierville, Tennessee

The Smoky Mountain Times, Bryson City, North Carolina

Asheville Citizen-Times, Asheville, North Carolina

The Knoxville News-Sentinel, Knoxville, Tennessee

Maryville Alcoa Times, Maryville, Tennessee

Books, Publications and Other Records

Smoky Mountain Historical Society Newsletters

U. S. Census Records

Blount County, Tennessee Marriages 1875-1910

In the Shadow of the Smokies, Cemeteries of Sevier County, complied by Smoky Mountain Historical Society

Records and files maintained by the National Park Service, and the Library at the Great Smoky Mountains National Park, Gatlinburg, Tennessee, open to the public under the Freedom of Information Act

Tax and real estate records in the counties of Sevier, Cocke, and Blount in Tennessee

Circuit and Criminal Court Records, Knoxville, Tennessee

Tennessee State Library and Archives, 403 Seventh Avenue North, Nashville, Tennessee 37243-0312

North Carolina Department of Cultural Resources, Division of Archives and History, 109 East Jones Street, Raleigh, North Carolina 27601-2807

Unsolved Mysteries, Post Office Box 10729, Burbank, CA 91510

Numerous Internet Web sites

Books About the Great Smoky Mountains
by Juanitta Baldwin
All the books are available at
http://www.amazon.com
and through bookstores

Smoky Mountain Ghostlore, ISBN 1880308-26-6.
The Smokies are home to ghosts - the land of adventures
and puzzlements. The book is a collection of legends,
personal encounters with ghosts, and folklore.

Smoky Mountain Mysteries, ISBN1880308185
This book is a collection of stories about the magnificent
Smoky mountains and their unique people.

Smoky Mountain Tales, Volume I, ISBN 978-1-
880308-27-1 ISBN before conversion to new system 1-
880308-27-4.

and

Smoky Mountain Tales, Volume II, ISBN 978-1-
880309-28-8, ISBN before conversion to the new system
1-880308-28-2

These two Volumes are a collection of true and tall tales
about life in the Great Smoky Mountains. Within their
pages, you will meet a throng of colorful characters. The
stories tell how life was in bygone days, and how it is now.

152

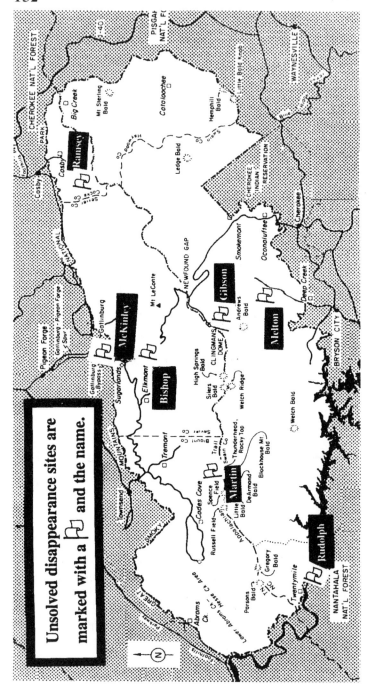